To:
_____

From:
_____

Date:
_____

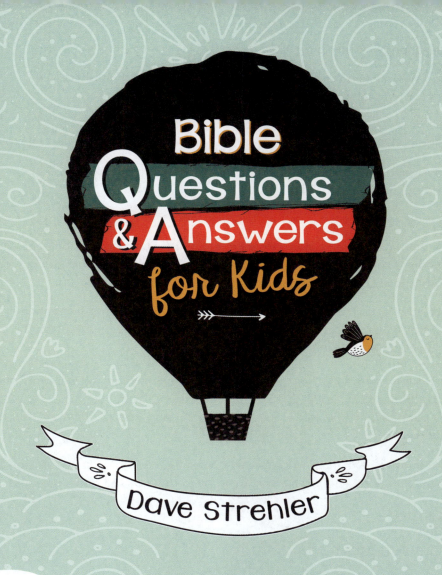

Bible Questions & Answers for Kids

Published by Christian Art Kids, an imprint of Christian Art Publishers,
PO Box 1599, Vereeniging, 1930, RSA

© 2021
First edition 2021

Cover designed by Christian Art Kids
Designed by Christian Art Kids

Images used under license from Shutterstock.com

Scripture quotations are from the Holy Bible, English Standard Version®. ESV® Text Edition: 2016. Copyright © 2001 by Crossway, a publishing ministry of Good News Publishers. Used by permission. All rights reserved.

Scripture quotations marked GNT are taken from the Good News Translation in Today's English Version – Second Edition. Copyright © 1992 by American Bible Society. Used by permission.

Scripture quotations marked NLT are taken from the *Holy Bible*, New Living Translation, copyright © 1996, 2004, 2015 by Tyndale House Foundation. Used by permission of Tyndale House Publishers, Carol Stream, Illinois 60188. All rights reserved.

Scripture quotations marked NKJV are taken from the New King James Version®. Copyright © 1982 by Thomas Nelson. Used by permission. All rights reserved.

Printed in China

ISBN 978-1-4321-3468-6

© All rights reserved. No part of this book may be reproduced in any form without permission in writing from the publisher, except in the case of brief quotations in critical articles or reviews.

23 24 25 26 27 28 29 30 31 32 – 14 13 12 11 10 9 8 7 6 5

Printed in Shenzhen, China
APRIL 2023
Print Run: PUR402999

To my grandson William

May God bless you with a deep longing
to know Him.
This is my prayer for you:
I pray that your love will overflow
more and more,
and that you will keep on growing in
knowledge and understanding.

Philippians 1:9

With grateful thanks to all the children
who submitted questions.

The following children gave me their names:

Karla
Michelli
Benson
Leyla
Mieke
Priscilla
Christie
Helen

Isaac
Valentina
Abiela
Paxton
Rafael
Becca
Andrew

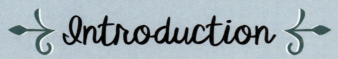

Introduction

When attempting to answer a child's question about the Bible, I always try to understand what he or she is really wanting to know.

While gathering some questions for this book, I was intrigued by a submission written on a small square of paper. It was this: *'Is there an answer for everything you ask?'*

So here is my reply to Michelli. Yes, there is an answer to every single question we can come up with. However, you may have a question that no one is able to answer. There are many, many things that even the experts don't know. Sometimes, the more we find out, the more questions we have. But be assured that God has the answer to every question. He knows everything about everything because He created everything!

God has given us His Word, the Bible. In it, we find all the answers to the important questions of life. This book aims to point you to Bible truths that will answer some of your questions and help you grow in your faith. **~ Dave Strehler**

God said,
"Call to Me and I will answer you,
and will tell you great and hidden things
that you have not known." JEREMIAH 33:3 (ESV)

The Quiz

At the end of every question there is a quiz.

- First, read the topical question and discussion.
- Next, read the quiz question and Bible verse. Then, mark the correct answer.
- Use the letter next to the square that you marked to complete the mystery page at the back of the book.

Contents

1. Who created God? 10
2. How big is God? 12
3. Can we see God? 14
4. Can God do anything?
   Can He bring dinosaurs back to life? 16
5. Does God have a body? 18
6. Does God care about me? 20
7. Does God know what I'm thinking? 22
8. Is God angry a lot of the time? 24
9. Does God ever get tired? 26
10. Does God laugh? 28
11. What does it mean God is a jealous God? 30
12. Where is God? 32
13. Why did God not just make us perfect? 34
14. Why did God make spiders and snakes? 36
15. Why did God need Adam's rib to make Eve? 38
16. Why did God make stars and planets we can't see? ... 40
17. Did God create the devil? 42
18. Is the world we live in now the same as the world
    God created? 44
19. Could God have created everything in just one day? ... 46
20. Were there dinosaurs in the Bible? Were they with
    Adam and Eve? 48
21. Is God still creating things? 50
22. God loves us so why did He make us on earth and
    not in heaven? 52
23. Why did the three wise men give Jesus
    such strange gifts? 54
24. Did Jesus cry when he was a baby? 56
25. Did Jesus have brothers and sisters? 58
26. Was Jesus still God when He was on earth? 60
27. Did Jesus make mistakes? 62

28. Did Jesus heal everyone?	64
29. Why did Jesus have to die to forgive us?	66
30. Did Jesus have special friends?	68
31. Why did people hate Jesus?	70
32. If Jesus came to save the world, why is it in such a mess?	72
33. Why did Jesus choose Judas to be a disciple?	74
34. Is the Holy Spirit real?	76
35. Can the Holy Spirit leave us?	78
36. Who wrote the Bible?	80
37. Why did people in the Bible get so old?	82
38. Why is there so much fighting in the Bible?	84
39. Why is there the Old Testament and the New Testament?	86
40. Why is Acts called Acts?	88
41. Why are there four Gospels?	90
42. What language did people in the Bible speak?	92
43. Did any women help to write the Bible?	94
44. Does the Bible talk about pets?	96
45. Who was the greatest person in the Bible?	98
46. In Revelation why does God's power seem so scary?	100
47. How can I have more faith?	102
48. What is the difference between a believer and a Christian?	104
49. If God knows what I need, why should I pray?	106
50. When should I pray?	108
51. Why do we close our eyes when we pray?	110
52. Where is heaven?	112
53. Does Peter let us into heaven?	114
54. Is hell a real place? What does the Bible say about hell?	116
55. Do angels protect us?	118
56. When I die do I become an angel?	120
57. Why will we get new bodies?	122

58. Why is life so hard?	124
59. Why does God let viruses take over?	126
60. When Adam and Eve sinned, why did God make more people?	128
61. If I do the same sin often will God stop forgiving me?	130
62. How can I forgive someone when I keep remembering what they did?	132
63. Why do we pray "lead us not into temptation"?	134
64. Is it a sin to get angry?	136
65. Will I be punished for my sin one day?	138
66. Why can't I be happy all the time?	140
67. I am scared of bad things happening. Can God protect me?	142
68. Do I have to obey rules that make no sense?	144
69. How do you know God is talking to you?	146
70. If God is everywhere, why do we have to go to church?	148
71. What should I do when I'm treated unfairly?	150
72. Is money bad?	152
73. Why can't we all just live in peace?	154
74. Did God ever use girls to do something great?	156
75. What did the Israelites use the ark for?	158
76. Will the world come to an end?	160
77. Is it wrong to have fun on a Sunday?	162
78. What is baptism?	164
79. Why are there so many different churches?	166
80. Are grown-ups always right?	168
81. How do you show God that you are thankful for what He has done for you?	170
82. How can we bless the Lord?	172
Keys to Every Book of the Bible	174

1
Who created God?

Many kids, and even adults, have struggled with the question of how things began. All of us have had a beginning, and we live in a world where everything has been either created or made. So it is hard for us to imagine how God was just there before time began.

God has always been God, and no one created Him. This is what God said, "I am the One who is, who always was, and who is still to come—the Almighty One."

When God spoke to Moses, He said, "I AM—that is My name." This name of God helps us to realize that He is in the past and the future at this very moment, because with God there is no time.

But what about us—do we have an end? Although we have had a beginning, those who have asked God to save them from their sin will go live with Him forever in heaven.

QUIZ 1

What did God call Himself?

Exodus 3:14

- **e** ○ 'I AM.'
- **r** ○ 'The God without beginning.'
- **m** ○ 'The God who always was.'

2. How BIG is God?

God is bigger than the universe! He is infinitely great, which means, God is everywhere—close by and far away at the same time (Jeremiah 23:23-24). He is bigger than anyone could describe with words. When we think about God, the only thing our words can do is worship His awesome greatness.

But the fact that God is so big doesn't mean that He won't notice you. Although adults may sometimes ignore you, God sees you and knows every detail about you. He cares for you and watches over you, day and night.

QUIZ 2

If God is so big, can He live in my heart?

1 Corinthians 3:16

- **d** ⬤ Yes, God lives in every believer through the Holy Spirit.
- **t** ○ No, my heart is too small for God.
- **s** ○ No, because God lives in heaven.

3 · Can we see GOD?

The Bible doesn't tell us of anyone who has seen God in all His glory. God is holy and we are sinful. If we were to see God, we would die instantly.

When Moses asked to see God's glory, God said to him, "No one can see My face and live." However, God did allow Moses to see His goodness by covering him as He passed by (Exodus 33:18-23).

Whenever God spoke to certain people in the Bible, they would only hear His voice. Some, like Jacob and the prophet Isaiah, saw a physical image of the invisible God, but they didn't see God Himself.

One day, when one of the disciples said to Jesus, "Lord, show us the Father." Jesus said, "Anyone who has seen Me has seen the Father" (John 14:9). In other words, if we want to know what God the Father is like, look at Jesus. Jesus came to earth as God in a human body.

So does that mean we will never see God? The good news is that, one day, those whose sins are forgiven will go to live in heaven and see God as He is (1 John 3:2).

⚜ QUIZ 3 ⚜

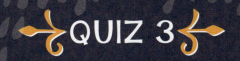

Can we see God?

Revelation 22:3-4

 ○ Yes, if we are very good.

 ○ No, we will never see God.

 ○ Not now, but one day when our bodies are made new in heaven.

Can God do anything?

CAN HE BRING DINOSAURS BACK TO LIFE?

The answer is YES ... if God wishes to do it. The answer is 'no' if it is something that goes against His character.

So if you ask 'Can God bring dinosaurs back to life?'

The answer is: YES, God can definitely bring dinosaurs back to life. He is the One who created every creature on earth. He created big ones, small ones, cute ones, and scary ones.

God can do absolutely anything because He is God. The chief angel Gabriel—who had seen God's power at work—said to Mary, "Nothing is impossible with God" (Luke 1:37).

There is, however, one thing God cannot do. God cannot sin. He cannot lie or do any other wrong. You see, God is not just all-powerful; He is good. That is why we don't need to be afraid of Him. We can trust God because He uses His power to help us—not harm us.

QUIZ 4

Can God bring a dead stick back to life?

Numbers 17:8

- **a** ○ No.
- **c** ○ Yes, if the stick is still on the tree.
- **d** ○ Yes, even if it is an old walking stick.

5 Does God have a body?

You may have asked this question because the Bible mentions certain human-like descriptions of God.

Here are some examples:

- **GOD'S EYES** (Psalm 34:15)
- **GOD'S MOUTH** (Isaiah 40:5)
- **GOD'S ARMS** (Jeremiah 32:17)
- **GOD'S HANDS** (Exodus 7:5)
- **GOD'S FEET** (Isaiah 66:1)
- **GOD HEARS** (Psalm 34:17)
- **GOD SITS** (Isaiah 40:22)

Word-pictures like these help us to understand more of what God is like.

However, God is Spirit, and so our eyes cannot see Him (John 4:24). That doesn't mean, though, that God isn't real, or that He is just some super-powerful force. What it does mean is that although we are limited by a physical body—God isn't.

QUIZ 5

Does God have a body like ours?

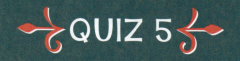
Numbers 23:19, Romans 1:19-20

- **g** ○ Yes, God is like us—just a lot bigger.
- **o** ○ No. God is real but different from us.
- **u** ○ No, God is not real. He is made up in people's imagination.

6

Does GOD CARE about me?

If you live in a large family, or a home where everyone is busy, it is natural for you to think that even God doesn't have time for you. After all, think of what it must be like to keep the whole universe going and answer everyone's prayers.

But God is not like us. We may be able to do a number of things at a time, but the more we do, the greater the chance of messing up. God doesn't need to rush from person to person to see if they're okay, or have someone write down all the prayers coming in just in case He misses one.

At any instant, God can name all the stars. Yes, each one of the billions of stars has a name! He can tell you the number of hairs on your head or grains of sand on the seashore. That's how great God is.

But more important than God knowing your name and every detail about you, is that He loves who you are. He cares how you are feeling, what you're thinking about, and what makes you worried or sad.

God's love for you is like a shepherd's love for his sheep (Psalm 23). You belong to the Great Shepherd; and if He should notice that you've gone missing, He would leave all the others to go look for you. He would search all over until He found you. That's how important you are to God! The prophet Isaiah said about God's tender care; "He tends His flock like a shepherd: He gathers the lambs in His arms and carries them close to His heart" (Isaiah 40:11).

QUIZ 6

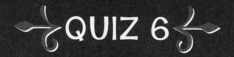

Am I as important to God as a grown-up?

Matthew 19:13-14

- **s** ◯ No, because grown-ups usually need God more.
- **n** ◯ Yes, you definitely matter just as much to God.
- **l** ◯ You are important to God, but some people like presidents, leaders, and kings come first.

7

Does God KNOW what I'm THINKING?

Hmm, that's a good one! The thought of God knowing your thoughts could be a little scary, especially if your thoughts do not honor God. But it could also be a great way to send God 'secret' prayer messages.

Let's see what the Bible says.

David wrote; "You know when I sit down or stand up. You know my thoughts even when I'm far away. You see me when I travel and when I rest at home. You know everything I do. You know what I am going to say even before I say it, Lord" (Psalm 139:2-4). That says it all! God knows all our thoughts, and even the exact words we will say.

But what about speaking to God with our thoughts? Hannah was a woman who desperately wanted a baby. So she went to the temple and prayed silently (in her heart). The Lord heard Hannah's silent prayer and answered it.

QUIZ 7

Can God hear my thoughts when I pray to Him?

Romans 8:26-27

- **n** ○ Yes, but only if it's absolutely quiet.
- **r** ○ No, God can't hear silent thoughts, so you should always pray aloud.
- **e** ○ Yes, God hears every word you are thinking, and He understands exactly what you're trying to say.

8
IS GOD *angry* A LOT OF THE TIME?

The Bible does talk about God's anger, but you should never think of His anger being like someone's angry outburst. "The LORD is compassionate and merciful, slow to get angry and filled with unfailing love" (Psalm 103:8).

Perhaps you've seen a painting of a god who looks angry, or been frightened by a thunderstorm, or read parts of the Bible that talk about God's anger. But these things should never make us afraid of God. God is never in a 'bad mood.' Even while He is angry with some, He delights in those who follow Him (Zephaniah 3:17).

So, what makes God angry? God is angry when people hurt others and treat them unfairly (Isaiah 10:1-3); when people lead believers away from the truth (Matthew 18:6, Romans 1:18), and when people disrespect His holiness.

QUIZ 8

Does God get angry when I do something wrong?

Psalm 103:10-14

- [x] No, God doesn't care about my sin.
- [v] No, because He knows that I am weak. My sin does disappoint God, but He loves me and wants to forgive me.
- [f] Yes, even the smallest sin makes God really angry.

9. Does God Ever Get Tired?

God can never get physically tired because He is a spiritual being. God is spirit (John 4:24). That means, God is very real, yet He is not limited by a physical body the way we are. He is infinite in every way!

However, you may be thinking, 'Why, then, did God need to rest on the seventh day of creation.' We think of needing to rest or sleep because we get tired. But when the Bible says God rested, it means He had finished working and enjoyed what He had made.

Spiritual rest is about relationship—God's relationship with us, and our relationship with Him (Matthew 11:28). That is why the seventh day, which is a day of rest, is about spending time with God.

Be assured, God's power never runs out. He doesn't get worn out and irritable, but remains patient and powerful to act. This verse says it all: "Do you not know? Have you not heard? The LORD is the everlasting God, the Creator of the ends of the earth. He will not grow tired or weary, and His understanding no one can fathom" (Isaiah 40:28).

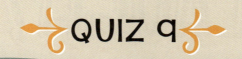

Did Jesus ever get tired while He was on earth?

John 4:6, Mark 4:38

- **b** ○ No, because God gave Him superhuman strength.
- **w** ○ We don't know for sure because the Bible doesn't tell us.
- **e** ○ Yes, Jesus was physically exhausted at times.

10 Does God ever LAUGH?

Can you imagine God laughing? Do you think He would laugh if He saw you slip in a mud puddle? It may surprise you that God does laugh, but not at people's misfortune.

God laughs at foolish people who think they are stronger or wiser than Him. He laughs at the wicked, for their day is coming (Psalm 37:13). He laughs at people who say there is no God because He knows that they will meet Him one day. Surprise!

How funny would it be if a tiny goldfish swimming round and round in a bowl thought he was the strongest and wisest creature in the whole world. It would be pretty ridiculous. Well, that's the way God sees people who think they've got it all.

QUIZ 10

Will we laugh in heaven?

Luke 6:21

- **o** No, because we won't be able to laugh.
- **e** Yes, because God promises to turn our sadness to laughter.
- **z** No, because we'll get into trouble.

11

WHAT DOES IT MEAN God is a jealous God?

I THOUGHT HE HAD EVERYTHING.

Yes, God does have everything.

God said, "Every animal of the forest is Mine, and the cattle on a thousand hills. I know every bird in the mountains, and the insects in the fields are Mine" (Psalm 50:10-11).

So what could He possibly want that He doesn't already have? God wants our heart's affection. He wants us to love Him with all our heart, soul, and mind (Matthew 22:37). God wants us to be loyal to Him and not love anything, or any one, more than we love Him.

The Israelites made God jealous because they started to worship idols and other gods (Deuteronomy 32:16). So God warned them: "Do not worship any other god, for the Lord, whose name is Jealous, is a jealous God" (Exodus 34:14).

God doesn't want things from us—He wants our love and devotion. He loved us so much that He sent Jesus to die in our place so that we can belong to Him. God longs to enjoy a close friendship with each one of us (Jeremiah 31:3).

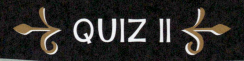

QUIZ II

If we put God first, does He mind when we enjoy other things?

Matthew 6:33, John 10:10

- [u] ○ No, God doesn't mind us enjoying life to the full.
- [t] ○ Yes, God becomes jealous when we have fun.
- [p] ○ Yes, God wants us to live a dull, boring life.

Where is God?

We know that God is everywhere, but perhaps you are wondering where He actually lives?

The most obvious answer is that God lives in heaven. There are verses that tell us about God sitting on His throne, for example, Psalm 47:8 and Isaiah 66:1.

When Jesus had gone back to heaven, one of His followers Stephen was stoned to death by angry people. Just before he died, he looked up to heaven and saw Jesus standing at God's right hand (Acts 7:55). That is just one way we know that God, and Jesus, are in heaven.

But heaven seems far away, and thinking about God being everywhere might not seem all that personal. That is why Jesus sent the Holy Spirit to live in the hearts of all those who believe in Him. Jesus said, "Anyone who loves Me will obey My teaching. My Father will love them, and we will come to them and make our home with them" (John 14:23).

God Himself answered our question when He said, "I am the high and holy God, who lives forever. I live in a high and holy place, but I also live with people who are humble and repentant, so that I can restore their confidence and hope" (Isaiah 57:15).

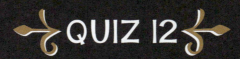

When does God come to live in us through His Spirit?

Ephesians 1:13

- **n** ○ When we are born.
- **h** ○ When we are old enough to pray.
- **l** ○ When we believe in Jesus and ask Him to save us.

13 Why did God not just make us PERFECT?

Then He would be happy and we would be happy

When we read the first two chapters of the Bible, we discover that God did make man perfect. Adam and Eve turned out exactly the way God wanted them to be, and God was pleased with how He had made them (Genesis 1:27-31). That was before Adam disobeyed God and caused sin to come into the world.

But perhaps you are wanting to know why God didn't make us perfect like the angels in heaven.

God wanted to make us different from angels—to make us in His image (like Himself). So God made us creative and gave us the freedom to choose.

Sadly, Adam used his freedom to sin and separate himself from God. But because God loved us so much, He already had a plan to save us and make us perfect again. He would send Jesus to die for us so that we could be made new on the inside.

QUIZ 13

Jesus will make our hearts new. Which part of us must we work on?

Romans 12:2

- [e] Our mind.
- [s] Our body.
- [a] Our soul.

·14·

Why did God make SPIDERS & SNAKES?

God created every creature with a purpose—to fit into His master plan. His plan was that everything in nature (plants and animals) should balance out perfectly.

In a perfect world—which God intended—animals and bugs weren't meant to harm us. That was before sin came into the world. Yet, even now that things aren't perfect anymore, scientists have discovered that every animal and bug has a purpose. Even spiders and snakes have their use in nature and keep other creatures from taking over.

In Bible times, God used gnats, flies, frogs, and locusts to punish the Egyptians and warn them to set His people free (Exodus 8-10). But it doesn't mean every mosquito is a punishment from God. So for now, in this not-so-perfect world, we just have to live with those 'nasties.'

QUIZ 14

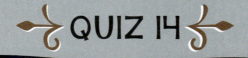

Is it wrong to kill one of God's small creatures?

Genesis 1:28

- **o** ⚪ It's okay to stop creatures from taking over or harming us.
- **b** ⚪ No, it's not wrong. We should kill all insects and reptiles.
- **g** ⚪ Yes, it's wrong! We shouldn't even kill a fly.

15. Why did God NEED ADAM'S RIB to make Eve?

Perhaps you are wondering why God didn't make Eve the same way He made Adam—by shaping her from the dust of the earth (Genesis 2:21-24).

If God had made Eve the same way He made Adam, they would have been two separate beings. Instead, God wanted their bodies to share the same cells (flesh and bone).

When God brought Eve to Adam, he was immediately attracted to her, and said, "This is now bone of my bones and flesh of my flesh; she shall be called 'woman,' for she was taken out of man" (Genesis 2:23). Adam had lost a rib, but in its place, he had something much better to complete him—a close companion. So when a man and a woman marry, the two become one in God's eyes.

Jesus said, "At the beginning of creation God made them male and female. For this reason, a man will leave his father and mother and be united to his wife, and the two will become one flesh. So they are no longer two, but one flesh" (Mark 10:7-9).

QUIZ 15

Was Adam awake when God took out a rib?

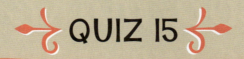

Genesis 2:21

- **l** ◯ Yes, that's how he knew that Eve was formed from the rib.
- **s** ◯ He was awake at first, but he passed out.
- **n** ◯ No, Adam was in a deep sleep when God took out a rib.

16. Why did God make STARS AND PLANETS we can't see?

Genesis, the first book in the Bible, explains that the world existed long before God put the sun, moon, and stars in their places (Genesis 1:14-18). So it almost seems as if God's focus was the earth—to make it perfect for us to live on. God decided to make everything around the world extra special—a bit like putting a beautiful frame around a painting. To God, creating billions of stars was as easy as it is for us to sprinkle glitter on something we've made. So it doesn't really matter that we can't see all the planets and stars.

Even before people had telescopes to see vast galaxies, they knew that the stars they could see were the magnificent handiwork of God. David, the shepherd wrote; "When I look at the night sky and see the work of Your fingers—the moon and the stars You set in place—what are mere mortals that You should think about them, human beings that You should care for them?" (Psalm 8:3-4).

Perhaps God created stars we cannot see so that we would realize how great and infinite He is and how small we are.

This psalm says it so well; "The heavens declare the glory of God; the skies proclaim the work of His hands" (Psalm 19:1).

QUIZ 16

Which came first, the sun or the stars?

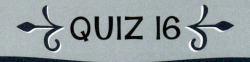

Genesis 1:14-19

- k ○ The sun was created first.
- n ○ They were created on the same day.
- a ○ The stars were created first.

17. Did God create the devil?

How did the devil become who he is, for we certainly know that he didn't create himself?

We also know that God created all things, through Jesus: "For in Him all things were created: things in heaven and on earth, visible and invisible, whether thrones or powers or rulers or authorities; all things have been created through Him and for Him" (Colossians 1:16).

Angels are created beings who worship and serve God. But the chief angel Lucifer (or light bearer) became so impressed with his own beauty and power that he wanted the glory that belonged to God. So God threw him out of heaven and down to earth (Isaiah 14:12-15, Ezekiel 28:12-17). His name was changed to Satan because he set himself up to be God's enemy.

God has never tempted anyone to sin (James 1:13). So, although God did create the angel Lucifer, He did not cause Lucifer (or the devil as we know him) to rebel and become who he is.

QUIZ 17

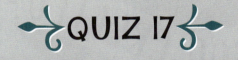

Does Satan still pretend to be an angel of light?

2 Corinthians 11:14

- **l** ◯ **No, he prefers people to know that he is evil.**
- **f** ◯ **No, because he doesn't want to be an angel anymore.**
- **s** ◯ **Yes, he tries to trick people and make them think that his ways are good.**

·18· IS THE WORLD WE LIVE IN NOW *the same* AS THE WORLD GOD CREATED?

If you live in a city, it probably seems like a totally different world to the Garden of Eden described at the beginning of the Bible. Maybe you've looked at a mountain range or picked up a jagged rock and wondered whether God created it exactly like that.

Over thousands of years, things have changed. Rivers have changed their paths over time, and mountains have lost a bit of their shape. Wind, water, sun, and fire change a landscape over the years.

People, too, have changed what the world looked like. Cities have been built and trees have been cut down. Much of the land has been shaped and changed to suit our needs.

Sin brought about the biggest change, and nature doesn't work quite as God intended it to.

You could think of the world like your favorite pair of jeans. Your jeans have probably faded quite a bit since you got them. Perhaps they now have a few stains; a tear in one place and a patch in another. Your mom may have altered them because you've grown. They're still the same, favorite pair of jeans that were once new, except that now they have a bit more character.

Yes, we still live in the same world God created thousands of years ago, and we should look after it as best we can.

QUIZ 18

What does it mean;
"God sent His Son to save the world?"

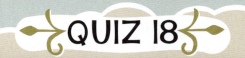

John 3:17

- **i** ◯ Jesus came to keep our world from spinning out of control.
- **r** ◯ Jesus came to save us from our sin.
- **j** ◯ Jesus came to help people understand the importance of nature.

19 COULD GOD HAVE CREATED everything IN JUST ONE DAY?

God is God, and that means He can do anything. So why did He need six days to create the universe?

It's not like God had to work late into the night to finish up before the next day. He simply spoke and things appeared. So He could have easily done everything in a day. Yet God is never in a hurry, but patiently puts His plans into action.

God is a God of order. He created everything in an orderly manner. He put natural laws in place (like the law of gravity and the law of energy). Although God can set aside those laws to fulfill His purpose, He usually makes things happen in line with those laws.

Perhaps God wanted to create only certain things each day so He could see how they work. Or perhaps He enjoyed creating so much that He just wanted to savor the joy of seeing things take shape.

Similarly, when Jesus used His power to heal people, He often just spoke a word of healing. Yet at another time, the healing was done step by step. For example, He said to one blind man, "Go, your faith has healed you" (Mark 10:46-52). He healed another blind man by first leading him out of the village and then letting him see just a bit before healing him completely (Mark 8:23-25).

There may also be another reason why God worked for six days and rested on the seventh. God was setting a pattern of what a week should be, and this pattern became an important command (Exodus 20:9-11).

QUIZ 19

Why does a week have seven days?

- **a** ◐ Because God worked for six days and rested on the seventh.
- **w** ◐ Because the Egyptians worked out the perfect number of days and weeks in a year.
- **m** ◐ Because seven is the perfect number.

20 Were there DINOSAURS in the Bible?

WERE THEY WITH ADAM AND EVE?

The Bible tells us a lot, but it doesn't tell us everything. It does, however, tell us all that God wants us to know.

The first book of the Bible tells us that God created livestock (tame animals), wild animals, and creatures that move along the ground (reptiles) - Genesis 1:24. It is possible that there were many kinds of animals living at that time that don't exist anymore. We know of animals that have become extinct even in our lifetime.

Job is an interesting book in the Bible. It tells of a man who lived after the flood. God spoke to Job, helping him realize that He, the Lord, is the One who created and controls everything in nature.

One of the examples the Lord used sounds a bit like what we may imagine a dinosaur would look like. Here's a description of the Behemoth: He eats grass as cattle do. His tail sways like a cedar tree. His bones are as strong as bronze, and his legs are like iron bars (Job 40:15-18).

If dinosaurs did exist, they would have been around with Adam and Eve because all the animals were created on the sixth day, together with Adam and Eve.

QUIZ 20

Where did animals get their names?

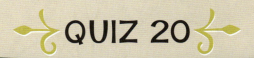

Genesis 2:19-20

- **r** ⭘ **Noah gave animals their names as they entered the ark.**
- **h** ⭘ **God let Adam choose a name for each animal.**
- **g** ⭘ **God chose a name for each animal when He created them.**

21

Is God still CREATING THINGS?

In Spring, when lifeless trees sprout blossoms and leaves, or when a baby is born, or a butterfly hatches from a cocoon, it seems as if God is still creating new life. Yet what we are seeing is His brilliant plan to let the life He created keep on re-creating itself in a natural way.

After the six days of creation, God did not keep on creating new kinds of animals and plants. When God had finished creating, He was pleased with what He had made. He was done, and nothing more was needed to make creation more perfect (Genesis 1:31, Genesis 2:1).

Right now, Jesus is holding all of creation together—including the atoms, the solar system, and the whole universe.

Although God has finished creating the physical world around us, He is still creating something beautiful.

God is giving new hearts to those who put their faith in Him. "And I will give you a new heart, and I will put a new spirit in you. I will take out your stony, stubborn heart and give you a tender, responsive heart" (Ezekiel 36:26).

QUIZ 21

Will God ever create something again?

Isaiah 65:17

- **e** ○ Yes, God will keep on creating different kinds of creatures.
- **f** ○ No, God has already created everything.
- **h** ○ Yes, God will create something new. But it won't be something in this universe. It will be a beautiful place, and it will last forever.

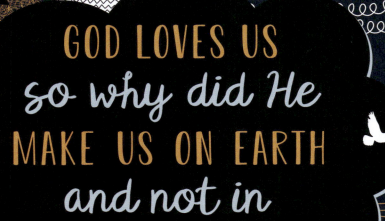

GOD LOVES US so why did He MAKE US ON EARTH and not in HEAVEN?

We, as humans, like to be close to the people we love. We are sad when we're separated from family and friends and we long to be with them.

But God is not human. He can be everywhere—in heaven and on earth at the same time.

God's plan was to enjoy being with us on earth. Before sin came into the world, God would speak to Adam and Eve in the garden. And even now, we can still pray to Him, and He can speak to our hearts through His Spirit and the Bible.

But why did God put us on earth in the first place? God created us with bodies that can enjoy His creation; emotions that can enjoy relationships, and a spirit that can enjoy His closeness. As we grow physically, emotionally, and spiritually, God is preparing us on earth for a special task in heaven (Matthew 25:21, Luke 12:44).

QUIZ 22

Who did God put in charge to rule the earth?

Genesis 1:27-28, Psalm 8:4-8

- **o** ⬤ Man (people).
- **s** ⬤ The angels.
- **n** ⬤ No one, because God doesn't want anyone to rule His earth.

23 Why did the three wise men give Jesus such strange gifts?

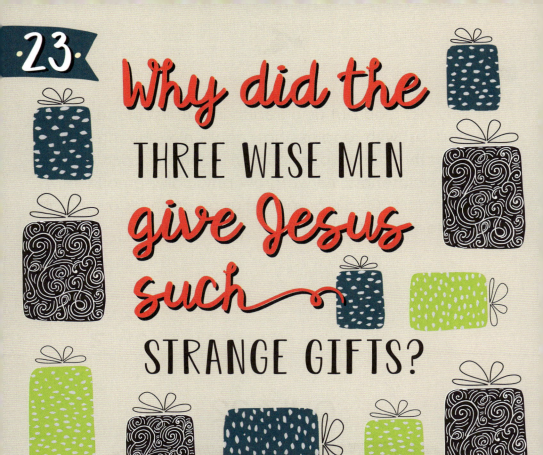

The gold, incense, and myrrh weren't just any old gifts the men brought along because they didn't know what else to give a baby. These were wise men who chose perfect gifts for a king. When at first the men saw the bright star in the east, they knew in their hearts that a great king had been born. They set out on a journey and followed the star to the place where Jesus was (Matthew 2:1-12).

The Bible doesn't actually tell us that there were three wise men. All we know is that the men brought three kinds of gifts. Each of those gifts had a special meaning.

Gold is a gift that one would give to a king because it is precious, pure, and beautiful. Jesus is the King of kings (Revelation 19:16).

Incense (frankincense) was an expensive perfume used by priests as an offering of worship. Jesus is our High Priest. Only He can make our hearts pure so that we can draw near to God (Hebrews 10:19-22).

Myrrh is a sweet smelling spice that was used on a body of a person who died. Jesus came to earth to die for our sin (1 Peter 3:18, John 19:38-39).

QUIZ 23

Who was the king of Judea when Jesus was born?

Matthew 2:1

- k ◯ King Nebuchadnezzar.
- w ◯ King Solomon.
- i ◯ King Herod.

24

Did Jesus CRY when he was a baby?

The Bible doesn't tell us much about the early years of Jesus, but it does tell us that Jesus was as human as we are. He was born the same way we were and grew up the same way we do. A baby's way of telling his mom that he needs something is to cry, so it would have been normal for Jesus to cry as a baby. And as a young child, Jesus had the same feelings all children have.

Even as an adult, Jesus cried when one of His friends died. As Jesus walked to the tomb where His friend was buried, He wept. He was heartbroken because of what had happened to His friend, and because He saw how sad the others were (John 11:33-35).

QUIZ 24

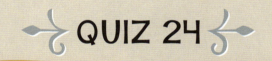

Does God know how many tears we cry?

Psalm 56:8

- **r** ◯ No, because He is busy sorting out bigger problems.
- **n** ◯ Our tears are precious to God. He counts every tear and will not forget our sadness.
- **d** ◯ Once we dry our tears, God can't see them anymore, and He assumes that everything is okay.

25

Did Jesus have BROTHERS and SISTERS?

Yes, Jesus was born into a normal family and had brothers and sisters. Jesus was Mary's first child, which made Him the eldest child in the family. Mary was married to Joseph, a carpenter in Nazareth.

We know that Jesus had four brothers; James, Joseph, Simon, and Judas, and at least two sisters (Mark 6:3).

Do we know whether they believed that He was the Son of God? It seems as if Jesus' brothers did not believe in Him at first (John 7:5), but after Jesus died and came back to life, His mother and brothers met for prayer with Jesus' disciples (Acts 1:14).

QUIZ 25

Did Jesus have other relatives His age?

Luke 1:30-36, 57-60

- [v] ◯ Not that we know of.
- [j] ◯ Jesus definitely had no relatives.
- [n] ◯ Yes, Jesus was related to John, the son of Elizabeth.

26

Was Jesus STILL GOD when He was on earth?

This question reminds us that God the Father, and Jesus, and the Holy Spirit are one. They are equal in every way, and all three are God. We call this the Trinity—**TRI**, which means three, and u**NITY**, which means one.

Jesus has always been God the Son. He was there before the world was created (John 17:5). Jesus was with God and He was God.

When Jesus came to earth, He humbled Himself and put aside His heavenly glory (Philippians 2:6-11). Jesus allowed Himself to be limited by a human body. He became hungry and thirsty and tired, just as we do.

So, was Jesus still God when He became human? Yes, He was still God in every way. He said to His followers, "I and the Father are one" (John 10:30). He also told them that those who have seen Him have seen the Father.

And what about when He died? When Jesus died on the cross, only His body (His human nature) died. His God nature did not die, for Jesus will always be God.

QUIZ 26

Was Jesus with God at creation?

John 1:1-2, Colossians 1:15-17

- **k** ○ No, Jesus watched from heaven as God created all things.
- **i** ○ Yes, God created everything together with Jesus.
- **y** ○ No, Jesus appeared for the first time when He was born as Mary's baby in Bethlehem.

We know that Jesus was perfect, but what does that mean? Perfect in God's eyes means being absolutely sinless, and that is what Jesus was (1 Peter 2:22).

Yet the Bible also tells us that Jesus had to learn things. Being completely human, Jesus had to learn to walk, and talk, and count, and read. Learning means that Jesus didn't know everything. For example, at the age of twelve, He stayed behind in the temple courts, listening to the teachers and asking them questions (Luke 2:41-46).

Jesus grew physically as a normal child does (Luke 2:52). Like us, He may have tripped, dropped things, mixed up words or cut the wood skew in His father's carpentry shop.

Even learning to be obedient was no easier for Jesus than it is for us (Hebrews 5:8). Yet Jesus wasn't disobedient once, because that would have been a sin.

There is a big difference between sinning and making a mistake. We may need to say sorry if we have spilled some milk or lost something and make things right, but we needn't ask God to forgive us if it was just a mishap.

QUIZ 27

Did Jesus go back to heaven with His human body?

Acts 1:9-11, Philippians 3:20-21

- [h] ○ Yes, Jesus went up to heaven with a perfect, glorious body, just like ours will be on the day He comes to take us to heaven.
- [n] ○ No, only Jesus' spirit went to heaven.
- [u] ○ No one knows because Jesus disappeared into thin air.

28. Did Jesus heal EVERYONE?

When we read the Gospels: Matthew, Mark, Luke and John, we discover some of the many miracles Jesus did. He healed the blind, the lame, the deaf, and the sick. Wherever Jesus went, there were always people who needed healing. Jesus felt very sorry for these people, and He healed them (Matthew 14:14).

But what if some of the sick weren't there that day, or they weren't able to get to Jesus as He passed by? That's what almost happened to a blind man.

One day, the blind man heard the noise of an excited crowd. When he asked what was going on, they told him that Jesus was passing by. So the blind man shouted for Jesus to have mercy on him. Then Jesus heard him and stopped. He told the people to bring the blind man to Him. Then Jesus healed him, and he could see again.

Perhaps if Jesus had gone a different way, or if the man had not called out to Jesus, he may not have been healed.

The people in Nazareth, where Jesus grew up, did not believe in Him. They said He was just an ordinary man. Sadly, because the people chose not to believe in Jesus, He could not do many miracles there, which meant that many sick people in that town were not healed (Matthew 13:54, 58).

QUIZ 28

Does the Bible tell us of all the miracles Jesus did?

John 20:30

- [w] Yes, every miracle Jesus did is in the Bible.
- [n] No, the disciples saw Jesus do many other miracles.
- [h] We don't know.

29. Why did Jesus HAVE TO DIE to forgive us?

In the Old Testament (before Jesus came to earth), the only way people could have their sins forgiven was for them to sacrifice an animal. The animal, which had to be perfect in every way, was to be brought to the priest who would kill it and burn it on an altar.

God cannot just forget about sin. The sin in our hearts doesn't just fade away over time. It stays there until God takes it away. Even then, something has to happen to the sin. In Old Testament times, God said that people could sacrifice an animal, and in this way the animal would die for the forgiveness of their sins. But the offering of animals was only a picture of what Jesus would do for us many years later (Isaiah 53:5-6).

Jesus came to earth to be a perfect sacrifice—to take our sin on Himself and die with our sin. By dying for the sin of the whole world, every one of our sins was buried with Jesus. And when Jesus was made alive again, the sin stayed behind because it had been paid for with His blood.

When the first man, Adam, sinned, God said that he would die. In the same way, every one of us has sinned and so we deserve death too. But Jesus died in our place. So now, everyone who is sorry for their sin and asks to be forgiven will one day live forever with God (John 3:16-18).

QUIZ 29

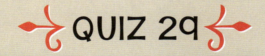

John 1:29

- k ◯ Jesus came to earth like a dove.
- e ◯ Jesus is the lamb of God.
- m ◯ Jesus is the white horse of heaven.

30 Did Jesus have SPECIAL FRIENDS?

We know that Jesus is a friend to everyone—even those who have done bad things. Jesus said to His followers, "I have called you friends and I have told you everything I have heard from My Father" (John 15:15).

But, did Jesus have some best friends? Yes, Jesus chose twelve men to be part of His team as He went around telling people about God. There were three men in that team who were really close friends. They were Peter, James, and John. They were the only ones Jesus chose to be with Him when He raised a little girl back to life; when He went up the mountain to meet with God, and when He prayed in the garden before He was arrested.

Jesus also had three other close friends. Whenever Jesus passed through the town of Bethany, He spent time in the home of Mary, Martha, and Lazarus, who treated Him as a very special guest.

QUIZ 30

Would Jesus care to have a meal with me and be my best friend?

Revelation 3:20

- **e** ◯ Jesus can't be a close friend to people anymore because He is in heaven now.
- **t** ◯ Jesus prefers to be friends with people who are really good.
- **s** ◯ Yes, Jesus is waiting for the invitation to come into your life and be your close friend.

31

Why did people HATE JESUS?

It is hard to believe that anyone would hate Jesus. He did no wrong and He hurt no one. Instead, He healed the sick, fed the hungry, and raised the dead. Jesus didn't even own anything that could have made people jealous.

So why did some people hate Jesus?

In the Old Testament, we see that people who lived sinful lives hated the prophets. The prophets warned that God would punish them if they didn't stop their sinful ways. But instead of listening to the prophets, the people beat them up and even killed them. Finally, God sent Jesus to earth—not an ordinary prophet, but His very own Son. Read the story that Jesus told in Matthew 21:33-39.

But the people hated Jesus, too, because He came as God's light to the world. Jesus explained why they hate what is good, saying, "Those who do evil things hate the light and will not come to the light, because they do not want their evil deeds to be shown up" (John 3:20 GNT). When sinful people see God's purity and goodness, they feel guilty. They want to put out the light so that they can carry on hiding in the darkness of their sin.

And so, these people spread lies about Jesus, argued with Him, and eventually had Him arrested and killed.

We should, therefore, not be surprised when others tease us for believing in God. Jesus said to His faithful followers, "A servant is not greater than his master. If people mistreated Me, they will also mistreat you" (John 15:20).

QUIZ 31

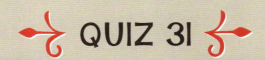

Even before Jesus was crucified, people tried to get rid of Him by…

Luke 4:28-30

- **q** ◯ **throwing Him into the Jordan River.**
- **j** ◯ **stoning Him.**
- **g** ◯ **throwing Him over the edge of a cliff.**

32 If Jesus came to SAVE THE WORLD, why is it in such a mess?

We first need to understand the Bible meaning of the world; and also, what you are thinking of when you talk about the world.

You may be thinking of this planet we live on, which David wrote about in Psalm 24:1: "The earth is the Lord's, and everything in it, the world, and all who live in it." Yes, many parts of this planet are in a mess because of man's selfish, careless way of life.

But there is another world that Jesus talks about in John 3:16: "For God so loved the world that He gave His one and only Son, that whoever believes in Him shall not perish but have eternal life." The world Jesus talks about is not the planet we live on, but rather, the people living on it.

Jesus came to save people from their sin so that they can have eternal life. But sadly, many people don't believe in Jesus and don't want to change the way they live. They prefer to carry on living sinful lives. Unfortunately, the sinful things they do often hurt others—especially those who are weak and helpless. That is why many people's lives are in a mess. Sin has brought disappointment, fear, sadness, and confusion. Yet in this messy world, the good news is that Jesus changes people's hearts, and He brings us life, hope, and joy.

QUIZ 32

Can we really make a difference in this sinful world?

Matthew 5:16, 1 Peter 2:12

- [i] ◯ Yes, we can be a light in this dark world by doing good and bringing praise to God.
- [m] ◯ No. Sin has made the world far too rotten.
- [b] ◯ There's nothing we can do because we are all sinners.

33. Why Did Jesus Choose Judas to Be a Disciple?

Jesus chose Judas as one of His team of twelve disciples. For three years, the disciples followed Jesus as He taught people about God and healed the sick.

One night, Jesus and the disciples were having a special meal together. Jesus, who knew what Judas had been planning, told him to go and do it (John 13:18-27). Judas left the room and went to carry out part of a deal he had made with the priests. They paid him thirty pieces of silver to lead them to Jesus (Matthew 26:14-16). Later that night, Judas led the men to the garden where Jesus was, and they arrested Him. If Jesus knew that Judas would betray Him, why did He choose Judas to be one of His friends?

Firstly, Jesus chose Judas because He loved him—not because he was perfect. In the same way, Jesus has chosen to love us. We may let Him down many times, or perhaps do something terrible, yet He loves us anyway.

Secondly, Jesus knew that His death was part of God's plan (John 3:16). Even if Judas had not betrayed Jesus, He would have still gone to the cross to die for our sins.

Thirdly, hundreds of years before, Zechariah had prophesied that Jesus would be betrayed for thirty pieces of silver (Zechariah 11:12-13). And that's exactly what happened.

God knows everything about us—everything we will say and do for the rest of our lives. Even so, we still get to make decisions because God has given us the freedom to make choices. Hopefully, you will always choose to do right. But even if you make a bad choice and do something wrong, God is ready to forgive you and help you carry on.

That's what happened to another disciple, Peter. The same night Judas betrayed Jesus, Peter denied Him three times. Although Peter loved Jesus, he was so afraid of those who had arrested Him that he said to others standing around, "I don't even know the man."

Jesus knew that Peter would deny Him, and Jesus also knows the worst about us; yet He has chosen each of us to be part of His team of followers.

QUIZ 33

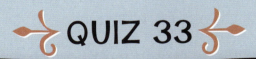

John 12:6, John 13:29

- e ⭕ He had to wash the disciples' feet.
- r ⭕ He had to prepare food for everyone.
- i ⭕ He was in charge of the money bag.

34. Is the HOLY SPIRIT real?

You may be wondering whether the Holy Spirit is like an invisible force or whether He is a real person.

The Holy Spirit is as real as God and Jesus. He is the third person of the Trinity. The Trinity is a word we use to say that the Father, the Son, and the Holy Spirit are equal, and that they are one. All three are God. The Father and Jesus and the Holy Spirit were together at the beginning and they created everything together (Genesis 1:2, Colossians 1:15-16).

The Holy Spirit now lives in the heart of every believer (Ephesians 1:13). What is even more amazing is that because God is three in one, Jesus lives in us (Ephesians 3:17) and God lives in us (John 14:23).

Although we cannot see the Holy Spirit, He is working powerfully in the world.

The Holy Spirit...

- shows us what is sinful and what is good (John 16:7-11).
- is a sign to those who are saved and a promise of what God has in store for us (2 Corinthians 1:21-22).
- helps us to become more like Jesus (2 Corinthians 3:18).
- helps us to understand the Bible (1 Corinthians 2:12-14).
- helps us to pray (Romans 8:26-27).
- comforts and strengthens us (John 16:7, Ephesians 3:16).

QUIZ 34

What is the temple of the Holy Spirit?

1 Corinthians 6:19

- **g** ⃝ The church.
- **e** ⃝ Our body.
- **u** ⃝ Heaven.

35 CAN THE Holy Spirit LEAVE US?

When we ask God to forgive us and make us new inside, the Holy Spirit comes to live in our hearts (2 Corinthians 1:21-22). Perhaps you are worried that if you do something really bad, the Holy Spirit might leave you.

In the Old Testament (before Jesus came), the Spirit of the Lord would come upon people whom God had chosen for a special task. There was Gideon the judge, David the king, Elijah the prophet, and others.

One day, David did a very bad thing. For a long time after he sinned, he didn't talk to God, and he felt far from God. But then he asked God to be merciful to him—to wash away his sin and make his heart clean. He also asked God not to take the Holy Spirit from him (Psalm 51:11). And God heard David's prayer.

But in the New Testament, things changed.

Just before Jesus went back to heaven, He had a long talk with His disciples. Jesus told them that the Holy Spirit would come and live with them as He had done (John 14:16-17). Soon after Jesus left earth to go back to His Father, the Holy Spirit came down on all the believers.

Unlike the Old Testament times when the Spirit only came down on certain people for a certain time, God has sent the Spirit to live in our hearts from the moment we give our lives to Him. In fact, God has put His Holy Spirit in our hearts like a permanent seal to show that we have been born again and now have eternal life (Ephesians 1:13).

You can be assured, even when we sin, the Holy Spirit will never leave us because our hearts have been made new and our names are written in God's Book of Life (Revelation 3:5).

QUIZ 35

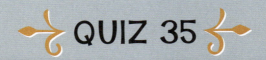

What should we do when we sin?

1 John 1:9, 1 John 2:1

- **I** ⚪ Try to forget about the sin.
- **n** ⚪ Confess our sin and ask for forgiveness.
- **c** ⚪ Make up for it by doing something good.

36. Who wrote THE BIBLE?

The short answer is, God is the author of the Bible. He chose certain people to write the words He put in their hearts. That's why the Bible is called God's Word. Though the prophets were human, they spoke the message from God as the Holy Spirit guided them (2 Peter 1:21).

The Bible was written by 40 people over a period of about 1,500 years. God used leaders, fishermen, kings, and prophets, as well as a doctor and a tax collector to compile His written Word.

Moses wrote the first five books of the Bible. David the shepherd wrote many of the Psalms. Luke the doctor wrote the Gospel of Luke and Acts.

Paul wrote letters to churches in different cities and areas, and these became part of the New Testament. He wrote to the Romans, Corinthians, Galatians, Ephesians, Philippians, Colossians and Thessalonians.

He also wrote letters to his friends Timothy, Titus, and Philemon.

The disciple John wrote the Gospel of John and the three letters, 1 John, 2 John, 3 John, as well as Revelation. Another disciple, Peter, wrote the two letters, 1 Peter and 2 Peter.

There were many other writers, and although they had different personalities and styles of writing, the message was the same. All 66 books fit together perfectly like chapters of one big book.

The Bible tells of God's love for man, our sin, and God's plan to save us from sin.

QUIZ 36

Did Jesus use scriptures that are now part of the Bible?

Luke 4:16-20, Luke 24:25-27

- **d** ◯ Yes, He showed people what the prophets said about Him and taught them from parts of the Old Testament.
- **r** ◯ No, He didn't need to use scripture.
- **v** ◯ No, because He didn't have an actual copy of the scriptures to read.

37. Why did people in the Bible get so old?

In Genesis, we read of people living to a very old age. Adam lived for 930 years; Noah lived for 950 years, and Methuselah lived for 969 years!

But then something happened. People became more and more wicked, and the Lord was sorry He had made them (Genesis 6:5-6). So the Lord said, "I will not allow people to live forever; they are mortal. From now on they will live no longer than 120 years" (Genesis 6:3 GNT).

And just as the Lord had said, people had fewer years on earth—fewer years to do evil and lead others into sinful ways.

blessing. Those who love and obey the Lord are blessed with many fruitful years on earth (Proverbs 10:27).

God already knows how many years each of us will live. All our days are written in His book (Psalm 139:16). Yet, more important than the number of years we live is how we live those years.

The Bible has this message to the young: "'Honor your father and mother'—which is the first commandment with a promise—'so that it may go well with you and that you may enjoy long life on the earth'" (Ephesians 6:2-3).

QUIZ 37

How old was Moses when he died?

Deuteronomy 34:7

- **t** ○ 120 years.
- **h** ○ 113 years.
- **d** ○ 100 years.

38. Why is there so much FIGHTING IN THE BIBLE?

Have you ever had an argument or a fight with someone? The first brothers in the Bible, Cain and Abel, had some trouble come between them. The Lord had looked with favor on Abel's offering but He did not accept Cain's offering. Cain got so angry that he killed Abel. That was the first fight and the first death in the Bible.

After some time, when there were many more people on earth, those living in cities were ruled by kings. It was only a matter of time before the kings ganged up to fight each other, and this meant that the people of those cities had to fight each other. This is how the first war started (see Genesis 14:1-2).

Years later when God's people, the Israelites, came to the land He had promised them, He told them to drive out the people living there. These were heathen nations that worshiped idols and did wicked things (Numbers 33:51-53). The Lord promised to help the Israelites drive the people out of Canaan. He would even use swarms of hornets to chase them out (Exodus 23:27-30).

God planned to rid the land of these godless people so that the Israelites would not mix with them and start doing the wicked things they did. But the people of Canaan stubbornly fought against God's people. Many of these battles are described in the books of Joshua, Judges, and 1 Samuel.

Once the Israelites had settled in Canaan, all would have gone well for them if only they had done a proper job of defeating the heathen nations. But they hadn't, and that led to further battles as those nations kept on attacking them from all sides.

What was worse, as the Israelites started to worship the heathen gods of those nations, their hearts turned away from God. After the Lord had sent many warnings through the prophets, He punished them by allowing the Babylonians to conquer them and destroy their land (2 Kings 8-12).

From these stories of war, we learn that it was the sinful hearts of people that led to all the fighting. Yet, even when God's people were outnumbered, they had amazing victories because God was on their side.

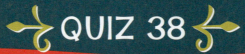

QUIZ 38

Who is our enemy now? 1 Peter 5:8

- l ○ The devil.
- o ○ Those who pick fights with us.
- a ○ Those who don't believe in God.

39. Why is there the OLD TESTAMENT and the NEW TESTAMENT?

The Old Testament and the New Testament are two parts of the Bible. Although the Old Testament is called 'old' it doesn't mean that it is out-of-date and no longer useful.

The Old Testament is about the old covenant (an agreement between God and man). The New Testament is about God's new agreement of grace.

The Old Testament

The first agreement that God made was with the nation of Israel. They were to obey the Ten Commandments as well as other rules. This was called the Law. If they kept the Law, God would bless their nation (Deuteronomy 4:1-2).

At first, the Israelites agreed to obey these laws (Exodus 24:7). But it wasn't long before they disobeyed God.

So God made another agreement with His people that, by faith, they could have their sins covered by sacrificing an animal (Leviticus 4:20). However, their sins would only be covered—not taken away (Hebrews 10:4).

The New Testament

After the first man Adam sinned, God promised to send a Savior to crush the devil's power over sin and death (Genesis 3:15). So, at the right time, God sent Jesus to die for us. He died as the perfect sacrifice to buy our freedom from the Law we couldn't keep, and adopted us as His very own children (Galatians 4:4-5).

This is God's new agreement with all people of every nation: that, by faith, anyone could have their sins forgiven (taken away) through the death of Jesus.

Both the Old and New Testaments are about a holy God who cannot overlook sin; yet a merciful God who longs to save sinners.

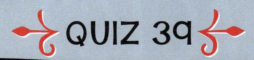

Is every part of the Bible useful?

2 Timothy 3:16

- **f** ○ Yes, every part of the Bible can teach us how to live a life that pleases God.
- **n** ○ We should only read the New Testament because it tells us about Jesus.
- **g** ○ Only the Old Testament is important because it has many exciting stories.

10. Why is Acts called ACTS?

Acts seems like a strange name for a book of the Bible. Some books are named after the person who wrote it, or the people to whom it was written. The names of other books describe what the book is about.

Acts is a short name for The acts of the Apostles. Another word for acts is actions—the deeds that were done.

When Jesus went back to heaven, He told the disciples to preach the Good News to all the world. Then Jesus sent the Holy Spirit to live in the hearts of all who believed in Him.

The disciples became known as the Apostles, and the book of Acts tells of all the things the Apostles did. They prayed, preached, healed the sick, helped the poor, started churches and spread the Good News of Jesus wherever they went.

QUIZ 40

Where would one find the book of Acts?

- [f] It is the last book in the Old Testament.
- [j] The book no longer exists.
- [n] It is the fifth book in the New Testament.

41 Why are there FOUR GOSPELS?

The Gospels: Matthew, Mark, Luke, and John are all about the life of Jesus on earth. They tell about the many things Jesus said and did. So, why four Gospels?

They were written by different people for different people. Although they are similar in some ways, there are some important differences.

Matthew, Mark, and Luke are called the synoptic Gospels because they are like a short story of Jesus' life on earth. John's Gospel is different because it tells us more about what Jesus said, especially to His disciples, than about the things He did.

Matthew, a disciple of Jesus, wrote an account of Jesus to the Jewish people. Being a Jew himself, he understood the way they thought and what they believed. The Jews were hoping that God would send them a king to free their nation from the Romans. So Matthew shows them that Jesus is the promised King, and explains how Jesus made many Old Testament prophecies come true.

Mark wrote to the believers in Rome. It was the first Gospel to be written, and it is also the shortest. This Gospel shows that Jesus came to earth as a humble servant, willing to help people and give His life to save them.

Luke, who was not a Jew, wrote this Gospel to those who didn't understand the Jewish faith and customs. He wrote down many of the parables that Jesus told, and he also helps us to see that Jesus was completely human, yet perfect. Luke, who was a doctor, added a lot of detail from his study of how things happened (Luke 1:1-4). He later wrote the book of Acts, which is like the second part of the Gospel he wrote (Acts 1:1-2).

John, a disciple and close friend of Jesus, wrote the Gospel of John. He was one of the first disciples and followed Jesus wherever He went. John helps us to understand that we are saved by believing in Jesus, the Son of God.

QUIZ 41

Do the four Gospels tell of everything Jesus did? John 21:25

- [**t**] ○ **Yes, the Gospels cover everything Jesus did.**
- [**l**] ○ **No, many more books could have been written about all the things Jesus did.**
- [**p**] ○ **There may have been a few things that weren't written down.**

42. What language did people in the Bible speak?

When we read the Bible, it is easy to think that the people spoke English.

Moses was the first person to start writing down the Word of God. He wrote exactly what God told him to (Exodus 34:27). Moses wrote in the language of his people, which was Hebrew. The old Hebrew alphabet had 22 letters and was written from right to left.

Most of the Old Testament was written in Hebrew, the language the Israelites spoke for over 1,000 years.

When Jesus was on earth, the language spoken in Israel was no longer Hebrew, but Aramaic. So you might think that the New Testament would have been written in Aramaic, but it was written in Greek.

Greek was the best language to use for writing and it was spoken by most people living in that part of the world. Latin was also spoken, but mainly by well-educated people.

When Pilate, the Roman Governor, had Jesus crucified, he fastened a sign on the cross. It read: "Jesus of Nazareth, the King of the Jews." The sign was written in three languages: Aramaic, Latin and Greek (John 19:19-20). These were the languages used in New Testament times.

QUIZ 42

Why did God mix up the language the first people spoke?

Genesis 11:1-9

- **o** God wanted people to learn more than one language.
- **e** God wanted people to learn to get along with each other in spite of their differences.
- **i** God wanted the people to stop building the tower of Babel. He made them speak different languages so they would move far away.

43. Did any women help to write the Bible?

'Help' was a good word to use in this question because people wrote what God put in their hearts. Although it was men who wrote down the words of the Bible, their writing includes the beautiful words of godly women. The exact words these women prayed and sang are in the Bible, and so in a way, they helped write those parts of God's Word.

Miriam - When God saved the Israelites from the Egyptian army by opening a way through the Red Sea, Miriam—the sister of Moses—played the tambourine and sang this song: "Sing to the LORD, for He is highly exalted. Both horse and driver He has hurled into the sea" (Exodus 15:21).

Deborah was one of Israel's judges (rulers). She encouraged the Israelites to fight against Jabin the Canaanite king. God gave the Israelites victory over the Canaanites, and on that day Deborah wrote and sang a victory song. You can find the words of the song in Judges 5:2-31.

Hannah was heartbroken because she could not have children. One day, she prayed for a son and promised to give him back to God. A while later, she became pregnant and had a son, whom she named Samuel. When Samuel was old enough, she took him to the temple where he served the Lord. On that day, she prayed a worship prayer about God's greatness (1 Samuel 2:1-10).

Mary - An angel appeared to Mary and told her that she was to be the mother of Jesus—the Savior of the world. When the angel had left, Mary went to her relative Elizabeth, where she sang a beautiful worship song to God (Luke 1:46-55).

These women help us to understand more about worship through song and prayer. Like Miriam, we can praise God who sets us free from being slaves to sin. Like Deborah, we can sing to God who helps us win our battles. Like Hannah, we can thank the Lord for answered prayer. Like Mary, we can glorify God for choosing us to be part of His plan.

QUIZ 43

Which two women are listed in the family tree of Jesus? Matthew 1:5

- **r** ◯ Sarah and Elizabeth.
- **a** ◯ Rahab and Ruth.
- **h** ◯ Rachel and Anna.

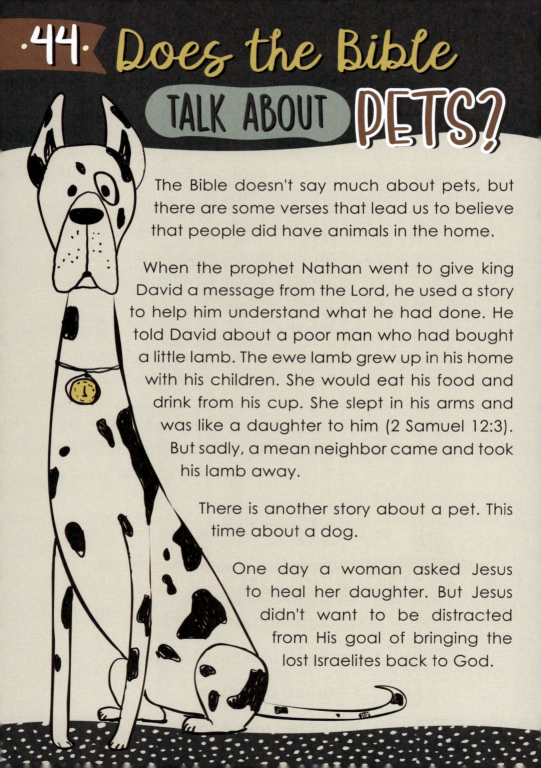

44. Does the Bible TALK ABOUT PETS?

The Bible doesn't say much about pets, but there are some verses that lead us to believe that people did have animals in the home.

When the prophet Nathan went to give king David a message from the Lord, he used a story to help him understand what he had done. He told David about a poor man who had bought a little lamb. The ewe lamb grew up in his home with his children. She would eat his food and drink from his cup. She slept in his arms and was like a daughter to him (2 Samuel 12:3). But sadly, a mean neighbor came and took his lamb away.

There is another story about a pet. This time about a dog.

One day a woman asked Jesus to heal her daughter. But Jesus didn't want to be distracted from His goal of bringing the lost Israelites back to God.

So He tested the woman's faith and said, "First I should feed the children—my own family, the Jews. It isn't right to take food from the children and throw it to the dogs" (Mark 7:27 NLT).

The woman, who was not Jewish, replied, "That's true, Lord, but even the dogs under the table eat the children's scraps!" The woman replied with such trust in the goodness of Jesus, that He honored her faith and healed her daughter.

Now, just in case you think that lambs and dogs were the only pets, James mentions how easily all kinds of animals were tamed. He wrote in his letter: "All kinds of animals, birds, reptiles and sea creatures are being tamed and have been tamed by mankind" (James 3:7).

So, yes, people in Bible times did love animals and kept them as pets.

QUIZ 44

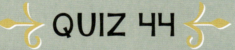

Proverbs 12:10

- [e] A righteous (godly) person.
- [k] A rich person.
- [d] An active person.

45. WHO WAS THE greatest PERSON IN THE BIBLE?

It is difficult to decide who the greatest person in the Bible was because we may have different ideas about what greatness is. For example, some might look at what a person did, while others may look at the person's faith or bravery. Without a doubt, we would all agree that Jesus was the greatest person who ever lived. His birth was a miracle; He was absolutely sinless; He did mighty miracles; His love was incredible, and He rose from the dead.

God used all those who were willing to serve Him, and each person was important in His plan. But perhaps, these Bible characters stand out for specific reasons:

Abraham had great faith, and he was obedient (Hebrews 11:8). He became the father of many nations.

Moses led a whole nation out of slavery to freedom. He also wrote the first five books of the Bible.

David was a songwriter and musician. He killed a lion and a bear with his hands and also slew the giant Goliath when he was young. He became Israel's greatest king.

Solomon was one of the wisest men who ever lived. He wrote many wise sayings called proverbs.

Esther's grace and bravery saved the Jewish nation from being wiped out when they were slaves in a far-away land.

Mary was the mother of Jesus. She was highly favored by God and has been called blessed by people through the years (Luke 1:28, 48).

John the Baptist. Jesus said that John was greater than anyone who ever lived (Luke 7:28). Perhaps it was because he was filled with the Holy Spirit from birth and because he prepared the way for Jesus' ministry.

Peter preached the first sermon about Jesus, and 3,000 people were saved (Acts 2:14, 41). He became the leader of the first church (in Jerusalem).

Paul the Apostle was the first evangelist. He spread the Good News in places where they had never heard of Jesus. He started many churches and wrote thirteen New Testament books.

QUIZ 45

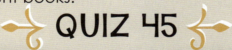

Who did Jesus use as an example of greatness in His kingdom? Matthew 18:1-3

- l ◯ A child.
- h ◯ A prophet.
- a ◯ An apostle.

46. IN REVELATION WHY DOES God's power SEEM SO SCARY?

Revelation is the last book in the Bible. It tells us what will happen in the last days—when the world finally ends and we go to live with God.

We are now living in the time of God's grace. That means God is inviting anyone and everyone to come to Him. Jesus has already paid for our sin. All we need to do is ask Him for forgiveness and follow His ways.

The Bible compares the end times to the days of Noah. People were becoming more and more wicked, and they didn't listen to God's warning. Instead of joining Noah on the ark and being saved from the flood, they carried on as if God didn't exist. Then the day of judgment came. God sent rain for forty days and forty nights, so the floodwaters rose; and it was too late for them to change their minds (Matthew 24:38-39).

One day, all those who love and obey the Lord will be taken from the earth. This will happen before all the terrible things in the book of Revelation take place (1 Thessalonians 1:9-10, 2 Peter 2:9).

Believers will be taken up to heaven in the clouds (1 Thessalonians 4:16-17). Only then will God's anger be poured out on the earth.

In the last days, Satan will realize that his time is short; and he will unleash his power against the people God created (Revelation 12:12). As God's power comes up against him, sadly, those who have sided with the devil will face God's anger too.

Although we should respect and honor the Lord, we should not be afraid of Him. He is our loving Father! "There is no fear in love. But perfect love drives out fear, because fear has to do with punishment" (1 John 4:18). We need not be afraid of God's punishment because Jesus has already been punished for our sin (Isaiah 53:5).

We now live in the hope of seeing Jesus return to fetch us when He comes in the clouds.

QUIZ 46

What are Jesus' last words to us in the Bible? Revelation 22:20

- [w] "Peace be with you all."
- [o] "I am coming soon."
- [y] "Blessed are those who stay faithful."

47. How can I have MORE FAITH?

To ask how you can have more faith means you already believe in God; and believing in Him is the foundation of our faith. "Without faith it is impossible to please God, because anyone who comes to Him must believe that He exists and that He rewards those who earnestly seek Him" (Hebrews 11:6).

Many of us long to have more faith—like the man who asked Jesus to heal his son and said, "I do believe; help me overcome my unbelief" (Mark 9:24).

Our faith can be strengthened by reading the Bible—hearing the Word of Christ (Romans 10:17).

When we read the Bible, we realize how powerful God is and how willing He is to help those who trust Him. But you may not have seen God doing big things in your life. Perhaps you've become discouraged and no longer expect Him to act.

By reading the Bible we learn that God is able to do miracles, and we are assured that He doesn't change. That means, God still hears and answers prayer in miraculous ways.

But if we don't ask God to help us, or expect Him to answer, our faith will remain small. We won't get to see how much God cares about our needs, and how willing He is to give His children what they ask (Matthew 7:9-11).

God has given us many promises in His Word! When we 'remind' God of a specific promise, we are asking Him to make that promise personal to our situation. Believe that God will make that promise happen in your life!

Faith is simply believing that God can do what we ask. He may answer in a different way from what you expect, but only because He has a better plan. Just trust Him!

QUIZ 47

What is faith?

Hebrews 11:1

- **m** ◯ Faith is wishing for something to happen.
- **g** ◯ Faith is being sure of what we hope for and convinced of things we cannot see.
- **s** ◯ Faith is saying positive words over and over till something good happens.

48. What is the difference between a *believer* and a *Christian?*

Both names were first used in the New Testament to describe those who have put their faith in Jesus. The names describe the same people.

The first people to put their faith in Jesus were called believers because they believed.

They believed:

- THAT THERE IS A GOD. *Hebrews 11:6*
- THAT JESUS IS THE SON OF GOD. *Matthew 17:5*
- THAT JESUS CAN SAVE THEM AND GIVE THEM ETERNAL LIFE. *Acts 4:11-12*

The first believers are described in Acts 2:42-44. They came together to pray and spent time learning from the apostles. They also shared what they had with others and gathered in homes to praise God.

Sometime later, the followers of Jesus were given the nickname 'Christian.' It was a name the unbelievers in Greece and Rome called those who followed Jesus. The name means Christ's one (or belonging to Christ).

Although the unbelievers used the name Christian as an insult, the believers were proud to be linked to the name of Jesus Christ. Peter said to his fellow believers, "It is no shame to suffer for being a Christian. Praise God for the privilege of being called by His name!" (1 Peter 4:16 NLT).

QUIZ 48

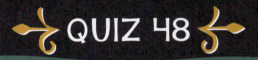

Where were the disciples first called Christians?

Acts 11:26

- [r] In Jerusalem.
- [n] In Antioch.
- [h] In Rome.

49. If God Knows What I Need, Why Should I Pray?

You may have read the verse where Jesus said, "Your Father knows what you need before you ask Him" (Matthew 6:8).

Although Jesus had just assured His followers that God knows their needs, He encouraged them to pray and ask God for their daily food (Matthew 6:9-13).

Usually, we have our daily needs provided for without even asking for them. But God wants us to ask for the things we often take for granted, like good food, warm clothes, and a home.

Asking God for our daily needs reminds us that we depend on our heavenly Father. Even though our parents may work to provide for us, without God's favor, we'd have nothing.

Asking keeps us humble because it means that we're not relying on our abilities only. We're relying on God, the One who has promised to care for us.

Asking the Lord, and thanking Him, means that we are talking to our Creator. As we talk to God, our relationship with Him becomes personal, and the more we talk to God the more we get to know Him and love Him.

As our heavenly Father provides for us, our response should be gratitude. Even when we thank the person who prepared our food, we should also remember to thank the Lord who sends the rain and makes things grow.

QUIZ 49

Did Jesus thank His Father before He fed a crowd of hungry people?

Matthew 14:19

- **z** ○ No, He didn't need to because He provided it.
- **b** ○ No, He didn't need to because the food wasn't for Him.
- **a** ○ Yes, Jesus thanked His Father for the food.

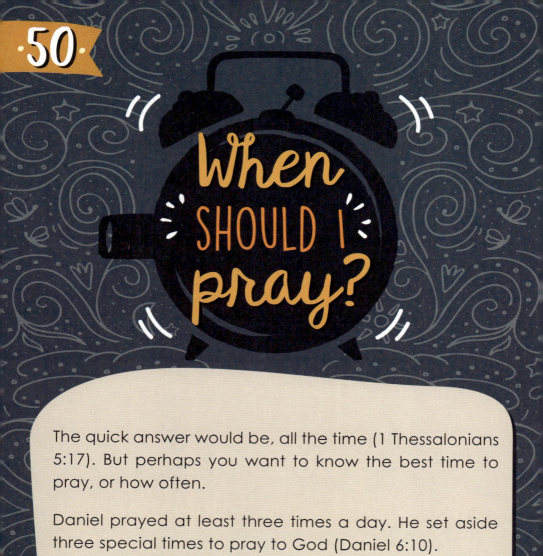

When should I pray?

The quick answer would be, all the time (1 Thessalonians 5:17). But perhaps you want to know the best time to pray, or how often.

Daniel prayed at least three times a day. He set aside three special times to pray to God (Daniel 6:10).

Early morning is probably the best time to pray because we can get our mind thinking about God, and leave all our cares with Him. Jesus often went out early in the morning to pray by Himself (Mark 1:35).

If you're not a morning person, you could get someone to wake you up a few minutes earlier. Go brush your teeth and then go pray somewhere quiet.

Praying at night before you go to bed is also a great time to think about the day, pray for forgiveness, and forgive anyone who has wronged you. Because you may have more time, it is also a good time to read your Bible and pray about what you've read.

However, God is there for you all the time. If you want to talk to Him at break time, or before a test, or on your way home, that's great! God is interested in every part of your life and wants to help you.

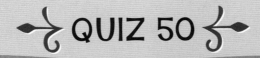

QUIZ 50

Should I carry on praying about the same thing? Luke 11:5-10

- **j** No, because we waste God's time when we pray unnecessary prayers.
- **c** You only need to ask God for something once.
- **e** God loves it when we talk to Him. He encourages us to keep praying and wait expectantly for His answer.

51. Why do we CLOSE OUR EYES when we pray?

The Bible tells us of people who stood and prayed (1 Samuel 1:26), sat and prayed (2 Samuel 7:18), and knelt and prayed (Acts 21:5). So it may surprise you that nowhere in the Bible does it say that people closed their eyes and prayed. If anything, Jesus sometimes looked up to heaven when He prayed (Luke 9:16).

Certain things like bowing our heads and folding our hands can show our respect for God and our humility.

Closing our eyes helps us to focus on God and not be distracted by the things around us. For example, if you were praying with your eyes open in your room, you may see a toy or a book and start thinking about all sorts of other things.

However, if your mind wanders more when your eyes are closed, you could go for a walk and pray or look out of the window while you pray.

QUIZ 51

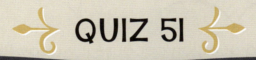

Is it okay to pray while I am busy at school or riding my bike?

1 Thessalonians 5:16-17, Ephesians 6:18

- [d] ○ Yes, we can pray anytime, anywhere— with our eyes open or closed.
- [u] ○ We should rather wait till we go to bed.
- [e] ○ It is better to pray in church on Sundays.

52 Where is HEAVEN?

That is a good question because if we say that heaven is above us, up is in a different direction depending where on earth you live. If you lived on the South Pole, 'up' would seem like 'down' to those living on the North Pole.

And yet, the Bible does talk about heaven being above us. For example, when Jesus left earth to go back to His Father, He went up into heaven (Mark 16:19).

So could heaven be all around the earth, like the sky? The Bible actually talks about three heavens. The first heaven is the atmosphere around the earth—the blue sky and the clouds. The second heaven is the universe, where the planets and stars are (Psalm 19:4,6). The third heaven is where God rules from His throne (2 Corinthians 12:2).

But before you start thinking how far away heaven might be, remember that we cannot see the spiritual world around us, so heaven may be closer than you think.

One day, when we go to heaven, our physical bodies will be changed. We will have a body just like Jesus—perfect and eternal (1 John 3:2), and we will live with Him in heaven, wherever that may be.

QUIZ 52

Is it possible that heaven is here on earth?

Psalm 102:19

- **l** ⚪ Yes. People living in a beautiful place talk about heaven on earth.
- **b** ⚪ The Bible does not tell us.
- **n** ⚪ No, because earth is sinful and heaven is perfect. God lives in heaven above us.

You may have heard people talk about Peter at the pearly gates of heaven, allowing in only those who deserve to enter. But that is not what the Bible says.

We cannot get into heaven by trying to be good enough—even if we try really, really hard. Only Jesus can take away our sin and make us good with His goodness. Jesus said, "I am the way and the truth and the life. No one comes to the Father except through Me" (John 14:6).

So why do people think that Peter is the one who lets us into heaven?

When Jesus was on earth, He said to Peter, "I will give you the keys of the kingdom of heaven" (Matthew 16:19). Jesus wasn't talking about actual keys to the gates of heaven, but saying that Peter would be used to tell people about God's plan to save them.

After Jesus had gone back to heaven, Peter preached to a large crowd. Thousands of those who heard Peter's message believed and were saved (Acts 2:38-41).

Just as a servant unlocks the door of a house to let a guest in, so Peter was given the task of opening the door of the kingdom so that people could come to God. The key to the door is the Gospel message—that God sent Jesus to save us from sin.

QUIZ 53

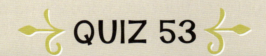

Are the gates of heaven really made of pearls?

Revelation 21:21

- **p** ◯ **No, but the color of the gates make them look like pearls.**
- **u** ◯ **No, because there are no gates.**
- **g** ◯ **Yes, each gate is made of a single pearl.**

54. Is Hell A *real place?*

WHAT DOES THE BIBLE SAY ABOUT HELL?

Jesus spoke with as much certainty about hell as He did about heaven. He told people about heaven and hell as being real places—heaven, where God is and where believers go when they die; and hell, where Satan will be doomed forever, together with those who choose not to believe in Jesus (John 3:18).

Yes, hell is a real place of unimaginable fear, agony, misery, and ugliness, from which there is no escape.

But why would God send anyone to hell? God's plan was to prepare a place of punishment for the devil and his angels (Matthew 25:41). But the Bible warns us, over and over, that anyone whose heart is sinful will follow the devil to hell, because sin cannot be allowed in heaven.

This is such a serious matter, that God was willing for His Son to die a cruel death so that we could be saved from our sin and go live with Him. He does not want anyone to be destroyed but wants everyone to repent (2 Peter 3:9). All we need to do is ask God to forgive our sins, and He will make our hearts absolutely pure and sinless.

QUIZ 54

Who holds the keys of death and Hades?

Revelation 1:18

- **a** ◯ Jesus, who died and now lives forever.
- **f** ◯ The devil.
- **j** ◯ The archangel Michael.

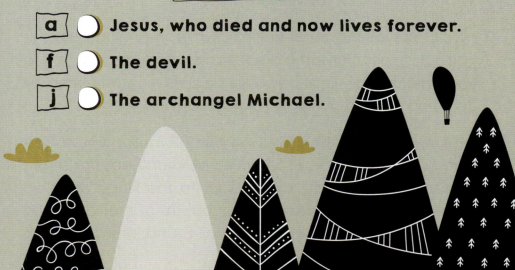

55
Do angels PROTECT us?

Because we can't see angels around us, you may wonder whether they really protect us.

Well, one of the most well-known stories in the Bible is about a faithful man called Daniel. He was thrown into a den of hungry lions because he disobeyed the king by praying to God. All night, Daniel sat with the lions.

In the morning, when the king and his men came to see what had happened to Daniel, he didn't have a single scratch on his body. Daniel said to the king, "My God sent His angel, and He shut the mouths of the lions. They have not hurt me, because I was found innocent in His sight" (Daniel 6:22).

Angels are sent to protect us physically and keep us from harm (Psalm 91:11, Psalm 34:7).

You have angels watching over you—angels who are told what to do by our heavenly Father (Matthew 18:10). God who knows exactly what will happen each day, tells His angels how to care for us. Even the youngest and the weakest and the poorest of God's children have angels protecting them.

But we should never pray to angels, but rather thank and praise the Lord who sends them. "Angels are only servants—spirits sent to care for people who will inherit salvation" (Hebrews 1:14 NLT).

QUIZ 55

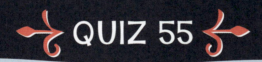

Can I expect God's angels to protect me if I cross a busy road without looking? Luke 4:9-12

- **y** ◯ Yes, the angels will keep you from getting hurt, even if you are careless.
- **d** ◯ No, God's angels cannot protect you.
- **e** ◯ God does send His angels to protect us from danger, but we must do what we can to stay safe.

When I die do I become an angel?

Maybe your mom calls you an angel, so it is easy to think of yourself as an angel in heaven.

Angels were created by God to be with Him in heaven. They worship God (Psalm 148:2) and are messengers from Him. They are also sent to protect people (Hebrews 1:14).

While we are on earth, we are a little lower than the angels (Hebrews 2:6-7). Angels are able to be in God's holy presence because they are sinless. They were created pure and good.

So what happens to us when we get to heaven one day? When we die, our spirit (the part in us that lives forever) goes to be with God.

One day, Jesus will come back to earth. All the believers who have died—as well as the believers living at that time—will get new bodies. We will go to live with Jesus in heaven, forever.

You will still be you, only a lot better! You will be perfect and sinless.

Although we will be with the angels, we won't be the same as them. Because we have lived on earth, we can understand things that they don't (1 Peter 1:12). We have been saved and have experienced God's grace. So, as part of God's plan to save us and make us perfect, we will be given the task of ruling over angels one day (1 Corinthians 6:3).

QUIZ 56

When we're in heaven, will we have a body like Jesus?

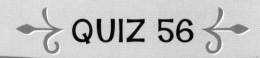

Philippians 3:20-21

- **a** ○ No, we will be more like angels.
- **t** ○ Yes, our bodies will be changed. We will have a glorious body like Jesus.
- **k** ○ No, we will have bodies like we have now.

57. Why Will We Get New Bodies?

Maybe you like yourself the way you are, and that's great because God made you that way.

You have probably heard, or read in the Bible, that we will get new bodies one day; and perhaps you'd actually like to keep the body you've got.

There is one problem, though. Everyone has been born with a sin-nature (Romans 7:18). That's why we do wrong things. Even though Jesus forgives our sins when we ask Him to, we are still stuck with our old sinful selves.

God cannot allow sin into heaven because He is holy, and heaven is His home.

But God loves us and wants us to live with Him. So He sent Jesus to die for us. When we ask Jesus to make our hearts new, He makes our hearts good with His goodness (1 Corinthians 1:30).

But because our bodies are sinful, we also need new, perfect bodies for our hearts. That is why God will give us a beautiful new body that can live with Him forever (2 Corinthians 5:1-5). In heaven, you will never get old, or feel pain, or be sad again!

QUIZ 57

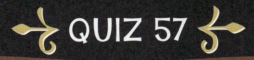

Will we have a special place to stay in God's home?

John 14:2

- **e** Yes. Jesus said that He is going to prepare a place for us and that His Father's house has many rooms.
- **u** We won't have our own place because one can't build anything in the sky.
- **m** We will probably just sit on clouds somewhere.

58. Why is life SO HARD?

We grow up in different countries; in different homes; with different families. We all have different abilities, and different strengths and weaknesses.

Some grow up in poor families; some grow up with everything they could wish for. Some are naturally sporty; some struggle to catch a ball. Some enjoy school; others hate school.

God Himself has fixed the exact times and places where people would live (Acts 17:26). He did this so that people would seek Him and find Him. In other words, God chose the right time for you to be born, and He put you in the right family so that it would be easy for you to get to know Him.

God also made you exactly the way He wanted you to be—with all the things you are good at, and also the things you are not so good at (Psalm 139:13).

God did not plan for us to sit around and do nothing all day. That would be boring. He planned that we should work, just as He does. God told Adam to look after the garden he was in (Genesis 2:15). So Adam had work to do.

Work was meant to be enjoyable for Adam, but after he disobeyed God, work became a chore. God's punishment was that Adam would have to work very hard just to make it through life (Genesis 3:17-19). He would experience failure and frustration.

If that's the way you are feeling, remember that God is there for you. He is with you all the time and will help you when you struggle. Just ask Him.

Jesus came to take away the curse of sin. Although God still wants us to work, we should see our daily tasks as working for Him. So, "Work willingly at whatever you do, as though you were working for the Lord rather than for people" (Colossians 3:23 NLT).

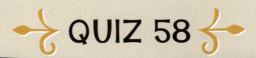

QUIZ 58

Which creature should a lazy person learn from? Proverbs 6:6

- **d** ◯ The donkey.
- **h** ◯ The sloth.
- **e** ◯ The ant.

59. WHY DOES GOD LET VIRUSES take over?

Viruses, and other diseases that spread, affect the lives of rich and poor; young and old; great and small. Sickness even comes to those who believe in God.

When God created the world, He formed all of nature beautifully. Everything was completely perfect (Genesis 1:31). There was no sickness and no death...until man sinned. Man's disobedience brought the curse of sickness, pain, and death into the world (Romans 5:12).

We now live in a broken world and face the challenges of our spoiled nature—where weeds (and viruses) keep on spreading (Genesis 3:17-18).

And because we, too, have sinned, we struggle through life with weakened bodies (2 Corinthians 4:16).

In recent years, a number of diseases have spread around the world through people's irresponsible actions. Some sicknesses are caused by eating unhealthy food; polluting nature, and doing things that are wrong.

But God doesn't want the world to be full of sick people. How do we know this? Jesus healed those who had leprosy and other illnesses (Luke 4:40).

God still heals and protects people today. We need not be afraid, because whatever happens to us, God holds us in His mighty hand. He will never let go of us! So, "Do not dread the disease that stalks in darkness, nor the disaster that strikes at midday" (Psalm 91:6 NLT).

There is another way God keeps us well. He has helped people discover cures and make vaccines. Today, there are medicines for all kinds of illnesses, and vaccines for most viruses, which means that we can live pretty healthy lives.

With bad news comes good news. Where diseases have spread right across the world, people have come together to help each other. Many have slowed down from their busy lives and had a chance to spend time on things that really matter. It has helped people focus less on themselves and care more for others.

QUIZ 59

When Jesus healed ten lepers, how many came back to thank Him?

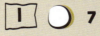

- **I** ○ 7
- **U** ○ 1
- **S** ○ 10

60

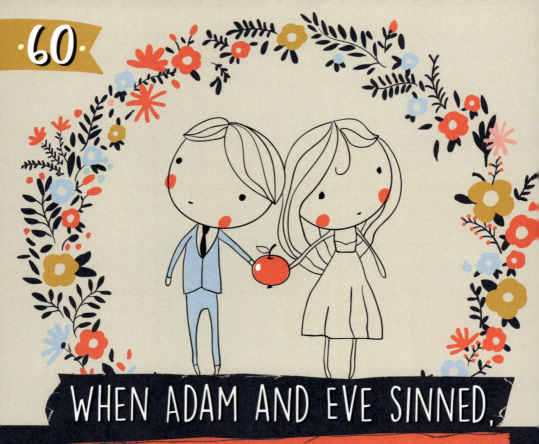

WHEN ADAM AND EVE SINNED, WHY DID GOD MAKE *more people?*

Sometimes, when we try something and it doesn't turn out the way we'd hoped, we may throw the idea aside and try something else. Perhaps you're wondering whether God could have just started over and made a new, perfect man and perfect woman.

God didn't make us to be like the animals He created. He made us in His likeness so that we could have a wonderful relationship with Him. His purpose for us was that He could love us, and that we would love Him. That's why God wasn't going to give up on His plan. Instead, as part of His plan, God sent Jesus to take away the sin that had come between Him and us.

Through forgiveness, which Jesus made possible on the cross, we can now draw near to God, and He can enjoy being close to us. "For the Lord your God is living among you. He is a mighty Savior. He will take delight in you with gladness. With His love, He will calm all your fears. He will rejoice over you with joyful songs" (Zephaniah 3:17 NLT).

Jesus is joyful over us too. He was willing to face the cross because of the joy that was waiting for Him—the joy of bringing us back to God (Hebrews 12:2).

QUIZ 60

Did Adam's two sons please God?

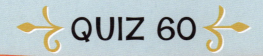
Genesis 4:3-8

- **b** ○ Adam only had one son, Cain.
- **u** ○ Adam's sons were equally bad. Both their offerings displeased the Lord.
- **d** ○ Abel did what was right in God's eyes, but Cain allowed sin to grow in his heart.

61. IF I DO THE SAME SIN OFTEN WILL GOD STOP FORGIVING ME?

None of us is perfect. As much as we want to be good, we find ourselves messing up and doing things that displease God.

Even Paul, the man who wrote many books in the New Testament, struggled to live a perfect life. This is the way he explained it: "I want to do what is good, but I don't. I don't want to do what is wrong, but I do it anyway" (Romans 7:19 NLT). Is that the way you feel sometimes?

God doesn't keep score of the number of times we sin. He will never say, "That's one sin too many; I can't forgive you anymore." God wants our hearts to be clean because He loves us and wants to be close to us. So, if you feel guilty and far from God, ask Him to forgive you. He will take away that heaviness from your heart.

It actually doesn't matter what you've done, or how often you've done the same thing. If you ask God to forgive you, He will. "If we confess our sins, He is faithful and just and will forgive us our sins and purify us from all unrighteousness" (1 John 1:9).

"Well then, should we keep on sinning so that God can show us more and more of His wonderful grace? Of course not! Since we have died to sin, how can we continue to live in it?" (Romans 6:1-2). If we deliberately keep on sinning, it shows that we aren't really sorry for our sin.

God wants us to grow in our love for Him and become more like His Son, Jesus. Here are some ways to stay away from sin:

- Read the Bible every day (Psalm 119:9-11).

- Pray that the Lord will help you win over temptation (Matthew 26:41).

- Don't spend time with friends that will drag you down (1 Corinthians 15:33).

- Keep your thoughts pure by filling your mind with good things (Philippians 4:8).

QUIZ 61

Knowing that God forgives us over and over, how many times should we forgive others? Matthew 18:21-22

- **t** ○ Seven times.
- **o** ○ 490 times, and after that keep on forgiving.
- **r** ○ It depends on what the person did.

62

HOW CAN I forgive someone WHEN I KEEP remembering WHAT THEY DID?

Forgiving is not trying to forget what someone did to you, or pretending it didn't happen. If someone hurt you or disappointed you, that feeling will probably stay for some time.

Forgiveness is choosing to let go of a grudge or anger against someone who wronged you (even if they don't deserve it).

Perhaps you have forgiven a friend but, somehow, you still feel hurt. Or perhaps something keeps reminding you of what happened.

If, however, you have forgiven the person, they are forgiven! So when a sudden bad feeling rushes in, or a memory pops back, remind yourself of the day you forgave them.

It may help to go and tell the person that you have forgiven them. Otherwise, write on a paper what the person did, and then tear the paper to shreds. Keep the pile of paper to remind yourself of the decision you made to forgive.

QUIZ 62

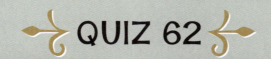

Matthew 6:14-15

- **c** ○ God still forgives us.
- **a** ○ God won't forgive the other person.
- **t** ○ God won't forgive us.

·63· Why do we pray "LEAD US NOT INTO TEMPTATION"?

When we pray the prayer Jesus taught His disciples (in Matthew 6:9-13), we are praying to God.

As part of this prayer, we are asking God not to lead us into temptation. But why would He tempt us to sin when He doesn't want us to sin?

The word temptation might be a bit confusing because we think of being pulled along into something that is wrong. Be assured, God would never do that to us! "For God cannot be tempted by evil, nor does He tempt anyone" (James 1:13).

Another word for temptation is a test or trial. What we are praying is that God will remember our weakness and help us not to be weighed down by our trial. We are praying that God will help us not to quit or compromise.

Knowing that we aren't able fight off temptation in our own strength, we have this assurance: "Every test that you have experienced is the kind that normally comes to people.

"But God keeps His promise, and He will not allow you to be tested beyond your power to remain firm; at the time you are put to the test, He will give you the strength to endure it, and so provide you with a way out" (1 Corinthians 10:13 GNT).

The second part of Matthew 6:13 helps us understand what we are praying in the first part of the verse. We pray that God will deliver us from the evil one. In other words, we are praying for God to come and rescue us when we are too weak to escape the enemy's grip.

Remember that temptation itself is not sin. Even Jesus was tempted. It is only when we disobey God and do what is wrong that we sin.

QUIZ 63

What should we do so we don't give in to temptation? 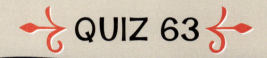 Mark 14:38

- **a** ◯ Keep watch and pray.
- **n** ◯ Stay busy.
- **i** ◯ Always be around other people.

64. Is it a sin to get ANGRY?

We all become angry at times for various reasons. We get angry when we are hurt, teased, disappointed or treated unfairly. Sometimes we also get angry because we are impatient or jealous.

Anger is your body's way of feeling—and often showing—that something isn't right inside. Something, or someone, has upset your peaceful heart, and your heart wants you to make things right.

Anger, love, joy, sadness, and fear are emotions—something we feel inside us, and that isn't wrong. God has made us to feel emotions.

While the feeling of anger is not sinful, the reason for our anger points to the problem. Some anger may be a natural reaction to protect a heart that is hurting. However, some anger is caused by selfishness. Pride, revenge or jealousy come from a heart that has a selfish attitude.

When our anger causes us to hurt others and destroy things, the reaction to those inner feelings is wrong. "Don't sin by letting anger control you" (Ephesians 4:26 NLT).

Forgiveness and understanding are the best ways to put out the blaze of anger and to mend a relationship. Trying to understand the way the other person sees a situation helps to calm things down. "Everyone should be quick to listen, slow to speak and slow to become angry" (James 1:19).

Can we use our anger for good?

We should only be angry at the evil that makes God angry. For example, if we are angry because we see someone being bullied, and we stick up for that person, we have used our anger to help someone. But remember to always take the proper action in a calm, controlled way.

Let this verse be your guide: "The LORD is compassionate and merciful, slow to get angry and filled with unfailing love" (Psalm 103:8 NLT).

QUIZ 64

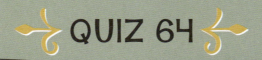

Whose jealousy and anger led him to kill his own brother? Genesis 4:8

- r ○ Samson.
- u ○ King Saul.
- n ○ Cain.

WILL I BE punished FOR MY SIN ONE DAY?

The good news is that if you have asked Jesus to forgive you, your sin is gone!

Maybe the thought crossed your mind, "What would happen if Jesus came back and I've just done something wrong?"

When we ask Jesus to save us from sin and give us eternal life, we become new inside. "Therefore, if anyone is in Christ, the new creation has come: The old has gone, the new is here!" (2 Corinthians 5:17).

The proof that our hearts have been made clean is that the Holy Spirit comes to live in us (Ephesians 1:13).

When we are saved, our spirit is made perfect in God's eyes, even though our body is sinful. "For by one sacrifice He has made perfect forever those who are being made holy" (Hebrews 10:14). In other words, Jesus has already made us perfect by taking all our sin on Himself and has made us right with God by putting His righteousness in us (2 Corinthians 5:21).

Although we will still slip up from time to time, our new heart will want to please God in all we do. However, if we do sin, we can ask for forgiveness and know without a doubt that Jesus will speak to the Father for us (1 John 2:1).

Jesus spoke these reassuring words: "Very truly I tell you, whoever hears My word and believes Him who sent Me has eternal life and will not be judged but has crossed over from death to life" (John 5:24).

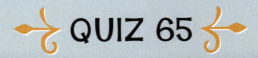

QUIZ 65

How far has God removed our sin?

Psalm 103:12

| e | ◯ As far as the sun is from the earth.
| y | ◯ As far as the east is from the west.
| f | ◯ As far as the north is from the south.

66

Why can't I be HAPPY all the time?

Being happy has a lot to do with what you expect from life. If you want to be the best, or the smartest, or the fastest, and you are not, you may feel beaten. If you want things to turn out exactly the way you planned, and they don't, you may feel frustrated.

Even when you do get what you want out of life, you'll find that the feeling of happiness will soon fade.

If, however, you are grateful for little things, and enjoy ordinary friends, and try to make a difference in this world, you may find that you will be happier and enjoy life more.

But happiness usually depends on circumstances—the things that happen around you. The world isn't perfect, and people aren't perfect, so things that go wrong are likely to change your normal level of happiness.

Joy has to do with relationships—not circumstances. The most important relationship is with Jesus, our faithful friend, who is with us now and will be for all eternity.

Joy also comes from the hope in our hearts knowing that, whatever we are going through now, the best is still to come. So be content with what you have, and accept the way God made you.

If your main goal in life is to be happy, you will probably never reach that goal; if your goal is to live a life that pleases the Lord, He will give you what you long for, and fill your heart with lasting joy (Psalm 37:4, John 15:10-11).

QUIZ 66

Which word is coupled with joy in a Bible verse? James 1:2-3

- [e] Popularity.
- [k] Riches.
- [d] Trials (troubles).

We live in a world where bad things happen. You may have heard reports of people being hurt or even killed. Things we hear can make us worry about our own safety.

There are three realities you can hold on to when you're afraid:

1. God is in control. Isn't it comforting to hear the words of your mother or father saying, "Don't worry, I am here." In the same way, God tells us, "I am the Lord your God who takes hold of your right hand and says to you, Do not fear; I will help you" (Isaiah 41:13).

God is always with you, protecting you from dangers on every side. The God of the universe is greater than all, and there is nothing He cannot handle.

2. God loves me. Your heavenly Father watches over you like a loving parent. That means, you are never alone!

Paul, who had a very difficult life and didn't know what would happen to him next, was able to say, "I am convinced that nothing can ever separate us from God's love. Neither death nor life, neither angels nor demons, neither our fears for today nor our worries about tomorrow—not even the powers of hell can separate us from God's love" (Romans 8:38 NLT).

We don't know what will happen to us in the future, but we know we are perfectly safe in God's strong hands. No one, but no one, can snatch you out of your heavenly Father's hand (John 10:28-29).

3. God promises to protect me. The Lord has the power to protect you, and He wants to protect you, and He has promised to protect you. The Lord says, "I will rescue those who love Me. I will protect those who trust in My name" (Psalm 91:14 NLT).

QUIZ 67

When I am afraid, I should... Psalm 56:3

- **c** ○ pretend to be brave.
- **d** ○ put my trust in God.
- **r** ○ tell myself to stay calm.

DO I HAVE TO OBEY RULES THAT MAKE *no sense?*

When we are told to do something—or not do something—we usually want to know the reason. Most times, we can figure it out for ourselves; and although we might not like the rule, we usually understand what it's about.

Rules are put in place to protect us; to protect others, and to protect property and the environment. That's why we have rules of a country, road safety rules, school rules, and even rules in the home. When playing a game, rules ensure that all the players are treated fairly. There are also unwritten rules—things we do out of courtesy and respect for others.

Rules and laws have been put in place over time for various reasons. Some have been around for so long that we may wonder whether we still need them. Yet, there is always a reason for the rule; and because it's a rule, we have every reason to obey it.

Does God expect us to obey rules that people have made? Yes! The Bible tells us to obey authorities—those who are in charge (1 Peter 2:13-17). We should also pray for them so that we can live peaceful and quiet lives (1 Timothy 2:1-2).

There is even an instruction (a rule) in the Bible just for kids. "Children, obey your parents in the Lord, for this is right. 'Honor your father and mother'—which is the first commandment with a promise" (Ephesians 6:1-2).

So remember to obey cheerfully, and encourage others to do so too.

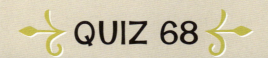

QUIZ 68

What man-made law in Bible times could never be changed?

Daniel 6:15

- [a] ◯ **The law of Moses.**
- [k] ◯ **The law of the Egyptians.**
- [t] ◯ **The law of the Medes and Persians.**

·69· HOW DO YOU KNOW GOD is talking TO YOU?

It is so important to listen for God's voice—like sheep who know their shepherd's voice (John 10:27). We hear many voices around us—in the classroom, at home, and on social media. So how do we know what God is saying?

Long ago, before there was a Bible, God spoke to certain people with a voice they could hear. But now God speaks to us through the Bible and the Holy Spirit in our hearts.

The Bible is the Written Word of God. That means it has been written down for us so that it will never be changed. It has been around for 2000 years and it is still the same Word that God gave us. By reading the Bible, we learn about God, sin, forgiveness, and many other things.

We, as believers, have the Holy Spirit living in us; which means, that as we read the Bible we grow in our faith (Romans 10:17). But more than that, reading the Bible is God's way of speaking to us, which makes it His Living Word (Hebrews 4:12).

As you read God's Word, the Holy Spirit makes the verses meaningful to your situation. In that way, God speaks to you personally.

For example, when you need God to guide you in order to make the right decision, He will show you what to do (Psalm 25:12).

Perhaps you are sad and need assurance that Jesus cares and knows how you're feeling. The Holy Spirit can comfort you as you read these and other verses: Psalm 34:18, Psalm 147:3, Revelation 21:4.

Maybe you're afraid or worried about something and you want to know that God is there for you. Look up these verses: Isaiah 41:10, Romans 8:28, Philippians 4:6.

Before you start reading from the Bible, ask God to help you understand what He is saying. Afterward, make time to think about what He has said to you.

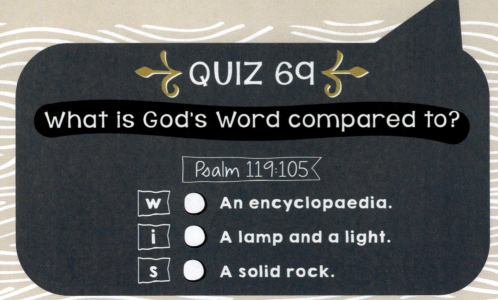

QUIZ 69

What is God's Word compared to?

Psalm 119:105

- **w** An encyclopaedia.
- **i** A lamp and a light.
- **s** A solid rock.

70. IF GOD IS EVERYWHERE, why do we have to go TO CHURCH?

In the Old Testament, the Lord told the Israelites to build a Tabernacle—a holy place—so that He could live among them (Exodus 25:8). When Jesus came to earth to die for us, He made us right with God. Now our bodies are the temple of the Lord. Jesus promised to be among us whenever a group of people get together in His name (Matthew 18:20).

Yes, it is true that God is everywhere, and we can pray to Him wherever we are. However, there are some important reasons that the Lord told His followers to gather together regularly.

Here are some things we can do better together:

- Worshiping the Lord as a group of believers can be meaningful and powerful (Colossians 3:16).

- We can hear good teaching that helps us to know the truth (1 Timothy 4:13).

- We can encourage one another and pray for one another (Hebrews 10:25, Matthew 18:19-20)

- We can build each other up by using our different gifts (Romans 12:6-8).

- We can bring some of the money we have as a love gift to the Lord (1 Corinthians 16:2).

Going to church shouldn't be a duty. Because we love the Lord, we should be happy to go and worship Him. As Psalm 122:1 says, "I was glad when they said to me, 'Let us go to the house of the Lord.'"

QUIZ 70

The church is... Ephesians 1:22-23

- [n] ◯ A building where religious people meet.
- [a] ◯ The Body of Christ—made up of those who are saved.
- [u] ◯ Any big place that is used for worship.

71. What Should I Do When I'm Treated Unfairly?

If there's one thing we learn early on in life, it's that life isn't fair. It wasn't fair for Abel, who was killed by his jealous brother. It wasn't fair for Esau, whose brother stole his inheritance. It wasn't fair for Joseph, whose brothers sold him as a slave. It wasn't fair for Jesus, who was beaten and crucified for us.

So how should we react when we are overlooked for a place on the team; when someone has more than we have, or when we're accused of something we didn't do?

The first thing we should do is check our attitude.

We should be humble and unassuming because pride lets us believe that we have a right to certain privileges and that we deserve special favor.

We should be thankful for what we've been given in life and learn to be grateful for small things.

So how do we manage our feelings of anger when we've been treated unfairly?

Let God handle the situation! He will judge the person or people who have wronged you, which means that you don't have to worry about getting even (see Romans 12:19). If anything, the very next verse tells us to do good to people who treat us unfairly because it will be like piling burning coals of shame on their heads. Ouch!

QUIZ 71

Whose unfair situation did God use for good? *Genesis 50:19-20*

- p ◯ Amos.
- j ◯ Moses.
- d ◯ Joseph.

72. Is money bad?

The Bible has quite a lot to say about money and riches. Jesus used money, and often talked about it, yet He didn't say that money is a bad thing.

Money is just an easy way to exchange our labor—the work we do—for something we need or want.

But money can be like a trap. It can lead down the wrong path when we long to have more than we need, or we do wrong things to get money. "Those who want to get rich fall into temptation and a trap and into many foolish and harmful desires that plunge people into ruin and destruction" (1 Timothy 6:9).

The problem isn't money, as such, which we need for everyday life. It's the love of money that causes all kinds of trouble. When money becomes more important than relationships, it brings out the worst in people and leads to jealousy, greed, selfishness, and pride. When money becomes more important than God, we break the first commandment.

Jesus said, "No one can serve two masters. Either you will hate the one and love the other, or you will be devoted to the one and despise the other. You cannot serve both God and money" (Matthew 6:24).

Here is some advice from the Bible:

Work for money (Ephesians 4:28)

Save money (Proverbs 21:20)

Be content with what you have (Hebrews 13:5)

Be generous (Acts 20:35)

QUIZ 72

What is more important than all the money in the world? Mark 8:36

- [g] ○ Being healthy.
- [k] ○ Your soul. (Whether you are saved and will spend eternity in heaven.)
- [k] ○ Having a good education.

73

Why can't we all just live in peace?

What a beautiful world this would be if there was peace on every continent. Everyone would be happy. There would be no arguing, no fighting, and no war.

The problem is that people are sinful, which makes us selfish and greedy. The Bible explains what the problem is: "What causes fights and quarrels among you? Don't they come from your desires that battle within you? You desire but do not have, so you kill. You covet but you cannot get what you want, so you quarrel and fight" (James 4:1-2).

The problem starts in our hearts. Unless we allow Jesus to change our hearts, our bad attitudes will keep leading to arguments and fights.

Jesus said, "Peace I leave with you; My peace I give you. I do not give to you as the world gives" (John 14:27). Once we have that kind of peace in our hearts, we will be happy with what we've got and happy to share with others.

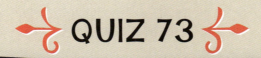

QUIZ 73

Can we be at peace with everyone?

Romans 12:18

- **e** ○ Yes. If we are nice to others, they will be nice to us.
- **h** ○ Not always, but we should do what we can to live in peace with everyone.
- **v** ○ No, people are selfish, so it doesn't help to try.

74 DID GOD EVER USE GIRLS TO DO SOMETHING *great?*

God uses anyone who is willing to do the things that please Him. Whether it is a big thing or a small thing, it is a great thing when we do it for God (Matthew 10:42).

When we think of children in the Bible who were used by God, we may remember the boy Samuel, who lived in the temple. One night, he heard God speaking to him. God gave him an important message to give to the priest.

Another boy God used in a big way was the boy who gave Jesus his five loaves and two fish. Jesus used the boy's lunch to feed over 5000 people.

But what about girls?

Miriam, a Hebrew girl, lived with her family in Egypt. The cruel king of Egypt had given an order that all the Hebrew baby boys be killed. Miriam's mom had just had a baby boy, and fearing for his life she hid him down at the river.

God used Miriam in a wonderful way to keep her baby brother, Moses, safe. When Moses was a grown man, God chose him to lead the Israelites out of Egypt to the Promised Land (Exodus 1:22-2:10).

Many years later, there was another young girl who was a servant in Naaman's house. We don't even know her name. Naaman was a powerful commander of the king's army. Yet he had a problem that even he couldn't tackle. He had a terrible skin disease called leprosy. One day the servant girl told Naaman's wife of a prophet in her home country Israel who would cure him of his leprosy. So Naaman went to see the prophet, and the Lord healed Naaman (2 Kings 5:1-2, 14).

God can use you too. If you think you are too young, take note of this verse: "Don't let anyone look down on you because you are young, but set an example for the believers in speech, in conduct, in love, in faith and in purity" (1 Timothy 4:12).

QUIZ 74

Which orphan girl became a queen who saved a nation? Esther 2:7, 17

- [ ] g Esther's cousin.
- [ ] m Esther's half-sister.
- [ ] r Esther.

75. WHAT DID THE ISRAELITES USE THE ARK FOR?

When God rescued the Israelites from slavery in Egypt, they had to walk through a desert to get to the land God had promised them.

While they were in the desert, God wanted to be near His people. So He gave Moses instructions to build a Tabernacle—a beautiful tent—where He could come down to be among them (Exodus 25:8). God also told Moses to have them make the Ark of the Covenant, which was to be a symbol of His presence and kept in the holiest part of the Tabernacle.

The Ark was a large box made out of beautiful wood and covered with gold. It was a reminder of God's covenant with the Israelites—that He would bless them if they kept His commands.

Inside the box were three important items (Hebrews 9:4):

The Stone Tablets on which the Ten Commandments were written. They reminded the Israelites of God's holy standard.

The Tablets remind us that Jesus was the only One who kept the commandments perfectly; and that by His death, we are set free from the law (Romans 8:1-2).

Manna in a golden pot. Manna was the daily food God rained down from heaven (Exodus 16:31-35). The pot of manna reminded the Israelites of how God cared for them and gave them food in the desert.

The manna reminds us that Jesus is the true bread from heaven (John 6:31-33).

Aaron's Staff. Aaron's walking stick showed that he and his tribe were the spiritual leaders (1 Chronicles 23:32). Aaron's staff was a dry, dead stick that God made alive. It budded like the branch of a young tree in spring.

The dead stick that budded reminds us that Jesus died for us and that God brought Him back to life (John 11:25).

QUIZ 75

What wood was used to build the Ark of the Covenant? Exodus 25:10

- [P] ○ Oak.
- [I] ○ Acacia.
- [W] ○ Cedar.

76. Will the World come to an end?

A lot of things need to happen before that, but yes, the world will eventually come to an end.

The disciples and Jesus were at the temple buildings when Jesus told them that not one stone of the walls will be left on top of another. The disciples were very surprised because the buildings were constructed with huge blocks of stone. So they asked Jesus, "Tell us, when will all this happen? What sign will signal Your return and the end of the world?" (Matthew 24:3 NLT).

Jesus told them that many things must happen before the world ends. One of the things is that the Gospel will be preached all over the world before that day comes (Matthew 24:14).

Ever since sin came into the world, the earth and nature have struggled along. "Against its will, all creation was subjected to God's curse. But with eager hope, the creation looks forward to the day when it will join God's children in glorious freedom from death and decay" (Romans 8:20-21 NLT). Nature waits for the day that it will be made new and perfect, just as we wait for the new bodies God has promised us.

This world, that has been so messed up by sin, will one day be destroyed, and God will make a new world. John the Apostle wrote, "Then I saw a new heaven and a new earth, for the old heaven and the old earth had disappeared" (Revelation 21:1 NLT).

God will make all things new! The end, as we think of it, will actually be the beginning of a new, perfect place for us to live forever with our new heavenly bodies.

QUIZ 76

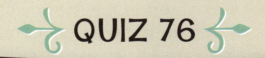

How did God destroy the world that existed when people became totally wicked? 2 Peter 3:6

- **a** ⚪ With tornadoes.
- **g** ⚪ With hail.
- **u** ⚪ With water.

77 · IS IT WRONG TO HAVE FUN on a Sunday?

The fourth commandment the Lord gave us says: "Remember the Sabbath day, to keep it holy" (Deuteronomy 5:12). For the Jews, the Sabbath day was on a Saturday, while believers in the New Testament changed their day of rest to the first day of the week, which is Sunday. Sunday is the day Jesus rose from the dead, and so it became known as the Lord's day.

The Lord said, "You have six days each week for your ordinary work, but the seventh day is a Sabbath day of rest dedicated to the Lord your God" (Deuteronomy 5:13 NLT). So what should and shouldn't we do on our day of rest? Well, we know that we shouldn't treat the Lord's day as an ordinary workday.

Instead, we should keep the day holy. That means, spending time with God—letting our minds think about Him so that He can fill our hearts with peace and joy.

The first disciples gathered together for worship, prayer, teaching; and to encourage each other in the faith (Acts 2:42-44).

The fourth commandment doesn't mean that we should be miserable and bored. Jesus said that the Sabbath was put in place for us—so that we have one day a week to rest and to spend with our Creator (Mark 2:27).

Of course, we can still do the necessary things, just as the disciples did when they picked and ate some grain on the Sabbath (Mark 2:23). God just wants us to put aside all our distractions for one day, and enjoy that day with Him.

Remember, your body also needs to rest for a day before the new week begins, but there's nothing wrong with having some fun too!

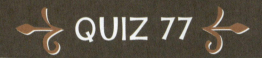

What does the Sabbath day mean?

Leviticus 23:3

- **f** ◐ A day for catching up on work that hasn't been done.
- **i** ◐ A day of rest and getting together with other believers.
- **t** ◐ A day to do absolutely nothing.

78

What is BAPTISM?

John the Baptist was chosen by God to prepare the way for Jesus. He baptized people who wanted to turn from their sin and follow God's ways. Baptism was a sign to others that they were sorry for their sins.

When Jesus was ready to start teaching the people about the kingdom of God, John pointed his followers to Jesus and told them to follow Him. Three years later, before Jesus left earth to go back to His Father in heaven, He said to His disciples, "Go and make disciples of all nations, baptizing them in the name of the Father and of the Son and of the Holy Spirit" (Matthew 28:19).

The baptism that Jesus spoke of is a sign that we have left our life of sin and have decided to follow Jesus. In other words, we have become disciples of Jesus—forgiven and changed on the inside.

A person who wants to be baptized goes into the water. Then the person who is doing the baptizing dips the person being baptized under the water for a moment.

Going under the water shows how your old life of sin has died and is buried. As you come up out of the water it shows how you have risen to a new life in Christ. "For you were buried with Christ when you were baptized. And with Him you were raised to new life because you trusted the mighty power of God, who raised Christ from the dead" (Colossians 2:12 NLT).

Baptism helps others to see and understand what has happened in your heart.

QUIZ 78

What did John the Baptist eat?

Matthew 3:4

i	◯	**Locusts and wild honey.**
t	◯	**Fish and figs.**
f	◯	**Vegetables.**

79

WHY ARE THERE SO MANY different churches?

You are probably familiar with your church and the way things are done there, but many churches are different and they have different names. Churches are usually given certain names to let people know where the church is, or to highlight a belief that is important to them.

The Bible tells us that the Church is the Body of Christ (1 Corinthians 12:27). That means, wherever there is a group of believers anywhere in the world, they form part of Christ's body and He is the Head (Colossians 1:18).

The church is not a building (even though we usually meet in a building). The church is made up of all those who believe and are saved. And so, believers in the New Testament are often called 'The Church.'

Perhaps your parents go to a certain church because it's where they've been going since they were young. Or perhaps they decided to find a church that suits your family best.

People sometimes choose to attend a particular church because of the truths that are taught there, or the kind of worship songs that are sung, or the program that is run for kids.

What matters is not what the church is called or where it is. What is important is...

that the Bible is taught there (Acts 11:25-26);

that there is love and unity between the members (Ephesians 4:1-6);

and that people are encouraged to tell others about Jesus and do good (Mark 16:15, Galatians 6:10).

QUIZ 79

Who wrote letters to the Church in Corinth?

1 Corinthians 1:1-2, 2 Corinthians 1:1-2

- [I] ○ Titus.
- [S] ○ Paul.
- [O] ○ Peter.

Are grown-ups ALWAYS RIGHT?

It would make sense that adults who tell you what to do and what not to do would, themselves, do what is right. Sadly, that isn't always so.

Parents, teachers, and leaders are human and get it wrong just as children do. They also make mistakes and do things they wish they hadn't.

Yet, the Bible tells us to obey our parents (Ephesians 6:1) and do what our leaders tell us to do (1 Peter 2:13), even though they are not perfect!

Children trust adults and believe what they say. They also understand that they should follow the example set by their parents. So when a parent does something that seems wrong to a child, it can be confusing.

Wrong doesn't become right just because the person is an adult! So if you feel in your heart that someone's behavior is wrong, then don't repeat what they've said and don't copy what they're doing. Every person must answer to God for what they do (Romans 14:12).

Because grown-ups sometimes get it wrong, it's best to follow Paul's advice if you believe that something doesn't please God: "Don't copy the behavior and customs of this world, but let God transform you into a new person by changing the way you think. Then you will learn to know God's will for you, which is good and pleasing and perfect" (Romans 12:2 NLT).

QUIZ 80

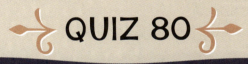

Can a young child be a good example to adults? 1 Timothy 4:12

- **e** ○ No, because children don't always know what's right and wrong.
- **d** ○ Yes, because children can touch the hearts of adults in a gentle way.
- **v** ○ No, because adults don't learn from children.

81. How do you show God that you are *thankful* for what he has done *for you?*

A thankful heart is an unassuming, humble heart. In other words, it is a heart that doesn't expect to get everything and understands when things don't work out.

The first way we can show God that we are thankful is to tell Him. There are many things we can be grateful for—even on an ordinary day. We can thank God for our health, our family, our friends, our home, and for daily food.

When we ask God for something, expect Him to answer, and thank Him. "Devote yourselves to prayer, being watchful and thankful" (Colossians 4:2).

The other way we can show God that we are thankful is by being kind to others. Jesus said that whenever we are helpful and kind to someone, it is as if we are doing it for Him (Matthew 25:40). In other words, we are giving back a little to say thank you for all the things we've been given, and that pleases God very much. "Do not forget to do good and to share with others, for with such sacrifices God is pleased" (Hebrews 13:16).

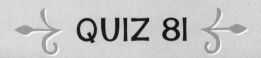

QUIZ 81

What was one of the ways people could thank the Lord in the Old Testament? Psalm 116:17

- **r** ◯ By celebrating Thanksgiving.
- **j** ◯ By saying certain words over and over.
- **h** ◯ By bringing a thank-offering to the Lord.

82. How can we BLESS THE LORD?

When we hear the word 'blessing,' we usually think of the Lord blessing us. For example, He blesses us by protecting us, helping us, giving us what we need, and by putting His peace in our hearts.

In the Old Testament, the Lord gave Moses a prayer of blessing for His people (Numbers 6:24-26); and in the New Testament, Jesus told His followers how God would bless them (Matthew 5:1-10).

Because God is the creator of everything, He has the power to bless His creatures. But how can we, as the people He created, bless Him? What do we have to offer Him?

Yet, Psalm 103:1 says;

Bless the Lord, O my soul;
And all that is within me,
bless His holy name!

God created us so He could love us and made us in His likeness so we could glorify Him.

We bless the Lord by worshiping Him with every part of us. Our worship pleases God when we have a clean heart, an obedient will, and a humble attitude that gives all the glory to Him (John 4:24).

We can bless the Lord by singing or speaking about His greatness and goodness (Psalm 34:1). We can lift His name high by telling everyone about the mighty God we serve (Psalm 145:1-2).

QUIZ 82

Is it okay to praise God if our hearts aren't right?

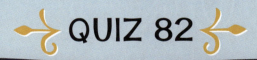

Isaiah 29:13, Psalm 66:18

- **u** ○ Yes. God is pleased with our praise even if there is sin in our hearts.
- **d** ○ We should ask God to forgive us and then praise Him with a pure heart.
- **s** ○ Because our hearts are so sinful, we should rather not praise a holy God.

Keys to every book of the Bible

Kids often ask why there are different books in the Bible, who wrote them, and where one should start reading the Bible.

Here is a bit about each book in the Bible and a key verse that you can try and memorize!

THE OLD TESTAMENT

ABOUT GENESIS

Genesis means *beginning*, and this book tells us how God created the world and everything there is. It also tells us how sin came into the world; why God sent a great flood, and where the nation of Israel came from. Genesis was probably written by Moses.

Genesis 1:1
In the beginning God created the heavens and the earth.

ABOUT EXODUS

Exodus means *to leave*. This book is about the Israelites being rescued from slavery in Egypt, and their forty-year journey in the desert with Moses as their leader. Exodus was probably written by Moses.

Exodus 15:13
In Your unfailing love You will lead the people You have redeemed. In Your strength You will guide them to Your holy dwelling.

ABOUT LEVITICUS

Leviticus gets its name from the tribe of Levi who were priests. In this book, God gives the Israelites instructions on how to worship Him. Leviticus was probably written by Moses.

Leviticus 20:26 (NLT)
You must be holy because I, the Lord, am holy. I have set you apart from all other people to be My very own.

ABOUT NUMBERS

The book gets its name from the counting of the Israelites in chapter 1 and chapter 36. Numbers is about the years that the Israelites spent in the desert. Numbers was probably written by Moses.

Numbers 6:24-26 (NLT)
May the Lord bless you and protect you. May the Lord smile on you and be gracious to you. May the Lord show you His favor and give you His peace.

ABOUT DEUTERONOMY

The name of the book means 'second law' because the rules God gave the Israelites are repeated. The book is about the last things Moses told the Israelites before they entered the Promised Land. Deuteronomy was probably written by Moses.

Deuteronomy 31:6
Be strong and courageous. Do not be afraid or terrified because of them, for the Lord your God goes with you; He will never leave you nor forsake you.

ABOUT JOSHUA

Joshua was the leader who took over from Moses and led the Israelites into the Promised Land. The book of Joshua tells of battles that were fought against the heathen people living in the land, and how the land was divided among the twelve tribes.

Joshua 1:8
Keep this Book of the Law always on your lips; meditate on it day and night, so that you may be careful to do everything written in it. Then you will be prosperous and successful.

ABOUT JUDGES
The judges were leaders chosen by God to help the people defeat their enemies. The book of Judges describes how God let enemies attack the Israelites because they began worshiping heathen gods. But whenever the Israelites turned back to God, He rescued them.
Judges 6:12 (GNT)
The Lord's angel appeared to him there and said, "The Lord is with you, brave and mighty man!"

ABOUT RUTH
This book is about a widow named Ruth who left the country where she'd grown up and followed her mother-in-law to the land of Israel. There she worked in a barley field to gather enough food for them. And that's where she met the man who would marry her.
Ruth 1:16
But Ruth replied, "Don't urge me to leave you or to turn back from you. Where you go I will go, and where you stay I will stay. Your people will be my people and your God my God."

ABOUT 1 SAMUEL
The people of Israel wanted a king like the other nations around them even though God was actually their King. So God let them choose a king. They chose Saul, but he disobeyed God and made a mess of things. So God chose a new king—David a shepherd, who killed the giant Goliath.
1 Samuel 2:2
There is no one holy like the Lord; there is no one besides You; there is no Rock like our God.

ABOUT 2 SAMUEL
This book carries on from 1 Samuel. It tells of all the things that happened while David was king of Israel—some good things and some not-so-good things.
2 Samuel 22:31
As for God, His way is perfect: The Lord's word is flawless; He shields all who take refuge in Him.

ABOUT 1 KINGS

Israel enjoyed a time of peace under the rule of King Solomon—one of David's sons. During this time, the Temple was built in Jerusalem. The book tells of Solomon's wisdom and wealth. But after his death, the kingdom of Israel was divided into two kingdoms—Judah in the south and Israel in the north.

1 Kings 8:23 (NLT)

O Lord, God of Israel, there is no God like You in all of heaven above or on the earth below. You keep Your covenant and show unfailing love to all who walk before You in wholehearted devotion.

ABOUT 2 KINGS

This book continues from 1 Kings with the history of Judah and Israel. It tells of the kings that ruled the two kingdoms until they were finally conquered by their enemies. The book includes amazing stories of two prophets, Elijah and Elisha.

2 Kings 17: 38-39

Do not forget the covenant I made with you, and do not worship other gods. You must worship only the Lord your God. He is the one who will rescue you from all your enemies.

ABOUT 1 CHRONICLES

Chronicles was written to remind the Jews—who had come back to their land—that they were still God's chosen people. It tells of people and events from Adam to the reign of King David.

1 Chronicles 16:11

Look to the Lord and His strength; seek His face always.

ABOUT 2 CHRONICLES

This book carries on from 1 Chronicles. It begins with King Solomon's reign and ends with the Israelites being conquered and taken as slaves to Babylon. The Babylonians also destroyed the temple in Jerusalem and took everything that was in it.

2 Chronicles 7:14
If My people, who are called by My name, will humble themselves and pray and seek My face and turn from their wicked ways, then I will hear from heaven, and I will forgive their sin and will heal their land.

ABOUT EZRA
After many years, when the Israelites returned to their land, they rebuilt the temple that the Babylonians had destroyed. Ezra taught the people, once again, to obey God's laws. Ezra wrote this book.

Ezra 8:23 (NLT)
So we fasted and earnestly prayed that our God would take care of us, and He heard our prayer.

ABOUT NEHEMIAH
The wall around the city of Jerusalem had been broken down by the Babylonians. When the Jews finally returned to Jerusalem, other enemies kept on raiding them. But Nehemiah had a plan. This book, written by Nehemiah, tells of the great job of rebuilding the wall around the city, and of all the things that went wrong.

Nehemiah 1:11 (NLT)
O Lord, please hear my prayer! Listen to the prayers of those of us who delight in honoring you.

ABOUT ESTHER
This is the story about Esther, a Jewish orphan, who stayed behind when many others returned to their home country. She was very beautiful and the king of Persia married her. A wicked man wanted to kill all the Jews still living there, but Esther risked her life to save them.

Esther 4:14
"For if you remain silent at this time, relief and deliverance for the Jews will arise from another place, but you and your father's family will perish. And who knows but that you have come to your royal position for such a time as this?"

ABOUT JOB

This book is about Job—a good man—who loses everything he had and then suffers from a terrible sickness. Job's faith in God is tested when his friends tell him that it's his fault that he is suffering. But God tells Job of His greatness and then gives him twice as much as he had before.

Job 19:25, 27
I know that my Redeemer lives, and that in the end He will stand on the earth. I myself will see Him with my own eyes—I, and not another. How my heart yearns within me!

ABOUT PSALMS

This is a collection of 150 songs and prayers that the Israelites sang. Some psalms are a cry for help while others focus on God's goodness and the great things He has done.

Psalm 55:22
Cast your cares on the Lord and He will sustain you; He will never let the righteous be shaken.

ABOUT PROVERBS

These are the wise saying of King Solomon and others. This book is a collection of practical advice about goodness, fairness, wealth, foolishness, pride, and many other topics.

Proverbs 18:10 (NLT)
The name of the Lord is a strong fortress; the godly run to Him and are safe.

ABOUT ECCLESIASTES

This book is about a search for the meaning of life. After looking at what some may think is important, such as pleasures and wealth, the writer advises us to remember our creator while we are young. Without God, life has no meaning.

Ecclesiastes 3:11 (NLT)
Yet God has made everything beautiful for its own time. He has planted eternity in the human heart, but even so, people cannot see the whole scope of God's work from beginning to end.

ABOUT SONG OF SOLOMON

This is a love song that shows how beautiful and pure marriage should be. The words are sung by a man to a woman, and a woman to a man, like a conversation.

Song of Solomon 2:4
Let him lead me to the banquet hall, and let his banner over me be love.

ABOUT ISAIAH

In this book, God sends Isaiah the prophet to warn His people of judgment for their unfaithfulness, and also warn other nations of judgment. But God also tells them about a coming King and Servant—the One who will saves us from sin.

Isaiah 41:10
So do not fear, for I am with you; do not be dismayed, for I am your God. I will strengthen you and help you; I will uphold you with My righteous right hand.

ABOUT JEREMIAH

The words of Jeremiah the prophet are written for us in this book. Jeremiah was chosen by God to warn the people about their stubborn hearts. He became very unpopular for saying that the Babylonians would conquer them (which they did). But in his message there are also words of hope.

Jeremiah 1:5
Before I formed you in the womb I knew you, before you were born I set you apart; I appointed you as a prophet to the nations.

ABOUT LAMENTATIONS

Lamentations are the sad words that describe the ruins of Jerusalem and the hardship of the people that were taken as slaves to Babylon. Yet, like a beam of light in the darkness, there is a hope that the Lord will have pity on them.

Lamentations 3:22-23
The faithful love of the Lord never ends! His mercies never cease. Great is His faithfulness; His mercies begin afresh each morning.

ABOUT EZEKIEL

Ezekiel was a prophet of God, who not only warned of God's judgment against Israel and other nations, but also speaks of the vision God gave him of the future Temple and the land.

Ezekiel 36:26 (NLT)
And I will give you a new heart, and I will put a new spirit in you. I will take out your stony, stubborn heart and give you a tender, responsive heart.

ABOUT DANIEL

Daniel, who was captured by the Babylonians, wrote this book while he was in Babylon. There he was chosen to serve the king. He was able to tell the king what his dreams meant, but he also ended up in a den of lions. Daniel had many visions about Israel's future.

Daniel 6:22
My God sent His angel, and he shut the mouths of the lions. They have not hurt me, because I was found innocent in His sight.

ABOUT HOSEA

Hosea, a prophet, was told by God to marry a woman who didn't love him. Although she was unfaithful to him, the Lord told him to take her back and love her just as He loves the people of Israel. This was to be a picture of Israel's unfaithfulness, and of God's unending love.

Hosea 6:3 (NLT)

Oh, that we might know the Lord! Let us press on to know Him. He will respond to us as surely as the arrival of dawn or the coming of rains in early spring.

ABOUT JOEL

Joel, who wrote this book, was a prophet of God who warned of locusts that would destroy the land. And so he calls on the people to turn back to God. He ends the book with a message of hope—that a time will come when God would give them back what the locusts had eaten.

Joel 2:13 (NLT)

Don't tear your clothing in your grief, but tear your hearts instead. Return to the Lord your God, for He is merciful and compassionate, slow to get angry and filled with unfailing love. He is eager to relent and not punish.

ABOUT AMOS

Amos was a shepherd who preached against the people of Israel (and other nations). He tells those who are rich and powerful to treat the poor with fairness, remembering that God rescued them from slavery in Egypt.

Amos 5:14

Seek good, not evil, that you may live. Then the Lord God Almighty will be with you, just as you say He is.

ABOUT OBADIAH

This short book, written by Obadiah, is a warning to those living in Edom (descendants of Esau) who were unwilling to help the people of Judah when they were captured and taken to Babylon.

Obadiah 1:15
The day of the Lord is near for all nations. As you have done, it will be done to you; your deeds will return upon your own head.

ABOUT JONAH

Jonah was called by God to go and preach in the heathen city of Nineveh. But Jonah disobeyed God and left on a ship going the other way. During a big storm, Jonah was thrown overboard. A great fish swallowed him and then spat him out on dry land. Jonah then got up and went to preach in Nineveh for 40 days. And because the people were sorry for their sins, God did not punish them.

Jonah 2:2
He said: "In my distress I called to the Lord, and He answered me. From deep in the realm of the dead I called for help, and You listened to my cry."

ABOUT MICAH

The prophet Micah wrote this book in which he tells the people in Israel and Judah that God would judge them for being unjust and proud. Micah includes a prophecy that Jesus—the promised Ruler—would be born in Bethlehem.

Micah 6:8 (NKJV)
He has shown you, O man, what is good; And what does the Lord require of you but to do justly, to love mercy, and to walk humbly with your God?

ABOUT NAHUM

This book, written by Nahum the prophet, begins by describing the greatness of God. It then goes on to foretell of His judgment on the city of Nineveh. (Once before, they had been warned of God's judgment and had repented. But some years later, they returned to their wicked ways.)

Nahum 1:7

The Lord is good, a refuge in times of trouble. He cares for those who trust in Him.

ABOUT HABAKKUK

The book Habakkuk is written as a conversation between the prophet and God. Habakkuk, who pleads with God to stop the violence and injustice in Judah, is surprised by God's answer—that He plans to use the ruthless Babylonians to do just that.

Habakkuk 3:17-18

Though the fig tree does not bud and there are no grapes on the vines... yet I will rejoice in the Lord, I will be joyful in God my Savior.

ABOUT ZEPHANIAH

The prophet Zephaniah, who wrote this book, tells of God's coming judgment on Judah and the nations. But there is hope: that the Lord will be merciful to His people. At the end of the book is a promise that God will bring the Israelites back to their land.

Zephaniah 3:17

The Lord your God is with you, the Mighty Warrior who saves. He will take great delight in you; in His love He will no longer rebuke you, but will rejoice over you with singing.

ABOUT HAGGAI

When the Jews returned to Jerusalem after 70 years in captivity, they started rebuilding their homes. But they got so busy with their own lives that they forgot about God's temple, which still lay in ruins. Haggai's short book is God's message to the people.

Haggai 1:7

This is what the Lord Almighty says: "Give careful thought to your ways."

ABOUT ZECHARIAH

Zechariah, the prophet of hope and comfort, called on Israel to return to the Lord. He had eight visions and spoke about things that are to happen on earth when the Lord returns.

Zechariah 4:6
"Not by might nor by power, but by My Spirit,' says the Lord Almighty."

ABOUT MALACHI

The book of Malachi begins with the Lord reminding the people Israel of His love for them. The prophet then calls on the people, and the priests, to do what God expects of them. For those who honor the Lord's name, a day is coming when they will jump for joy—free as calves let out of a stall.

Malachi 4:2
But for you who revere My name, the Sun of Righteousness will rise with healing in its rays. And you will go out and frolic like well-fed calves.

THE NEW TESTAMENT

ABOUT MATTHEW

Matthew, a disciple, wrote this account of Jesus' life on earth. He wanted the Jewish readers to know that Jesus is the Messiah—the King they'd been waiting for. He starts with the birth of Jesus and ends with Jesus rising from the dead and sending His disciples out to spread the Good News.

Matthew 11:28
Come to Me, all you who are weary and burdened, and I will give you rest.

ABOUT MARK

This action-packed Gospel was probably the first to be written. The book helps us to see that although Jesus came as a servant, He had His Father's authority to do miracles, proving that He is the Son of God.

Mark 10:27
Jesus looked at them and said, "With man this is impossible, but not with God; all things are possible with God."

ABOUT LUKE
Luke, a doctor, wrote this book. It was mainly written to Greek readers to show that Jesus came to save us from sin. This book includes many of the parables that Jesus told, as well as the family-tree of Jesus going right back to Adam.

Luke 19:10
For the Son of Man came to seek and to save the lost.

ABOUT JOHN
In this book, John—a close disciple of Jesus—writes down the things he saw Jesus do and the things he heard Jesus say. His message is that Jesus, the Son of God, is the only way to have eternal life. Half of the book is about the last few weeks of Jesus' life on earth.

John 3:16-17
For God so loved the world that He gave His one and only Son, that whoever believes in Him shall not perish but have eternal life. For God did not send His Son into the world to condemn the world, but to save the world through Him.

ABOUT ACTS
Acts is a short name for the Acts of the Apostles. Luke wrote this book, which follows on from the Gospel of Luke. This book is about how the Church grew and spread after Jesus returned to heaven and the Holy Spirit came down on all believers. Peter is the main character in the first part, while Paul becomes the main character as the Church spread to other parts of the world.

Acts 16:31
Believe in the Lord Jesus, and you will be saved—you and your household.

ABOUT ROMANS
This book is a letter that Paul wrote to the believers in Rome. In it, he explains that our righteousness (our goodness in the sight of God) comes from God Himself. We are made right with God by placing our faith in Jesus Christ our Savior.

Romans 8:28
And we know that in all things God works for the good of those who love Him, who have been called according to His purpose.

ABOUT 1 CORINTHIANS

Paul wrote this letter to the believers living in the city of Corinth. In his letter, Paul answers some questions about how Christians should behave. He also tries to bring together a divided Church by pointing out that the most important gift God has given us is love.

1 Corinthians 13:4-5

Love is patient, love is kind. It does not envy, it does not boast, it is not proud. It does not dishonor others, it is not self-seeking, it is not easily angered, it keeps no record of wrongs.

ABOUT 2 CORINTHIANS

Paul wrote this second letter to the church in Corinth while he was in Macedonia. After Paul's first letter, most of the believers had changed their ways, but Paul needed to tell those who refused to listen to him that he speaks with the authority that Christ has given him.

2 Corinthians 5:17

Therefore, if anyone is in Christ, the new creation has come: The old has gone, the new is here!

ABOUT GALATIANS

This is a letter Paul wrote to the Christians in Galatia, many of whom were Jews. They wanted to hold on to their Jewish customs as part of their faith. So Paul tells them that we can only be saved by faith in Jesus Christ—not by trying to obey the law in the hope of improving ourselves in God's eyes.

Galatians 5:22-23

But the fruit of the Spirit is love, joy, peace, forbearance, kindness, goodness, faithfulness, gentleness and self-control. Against such things there is no law.

ABOUT EPHESIANS

Paul wrote this letter from a prison in Rome to strengthen the faith of the believers in Ephesus and to encourage them. From there, the letter was probably sent to other churches in Asia.

Ephesians 2:10

For we are God's handiwork, created in Christ Jesus to do good works, which God prepared in advance for us to do.

ABOUT PHILIPPIANS

This is a thank you letter from Paul to the church in Philippi for the money they had sent him. Paul also uses the opportunity to strengthen and encourage the believers in their faith.

Philippians 4:6

Do not be anxious about anything, but in every situation, by prayer and petition, with thanksgiving, present your requests to God.

ABOUT COLOSSIANS

Paul wrote this letter to correct some wrong thinking the Colossians had about Christ. He reminds them about the greatness of Christ: that He is like God in every way; that He is the creator of everything; that He was there before creation; and that He is the Head of the body – the Church.

Colossians 3:15

Let the peace of Christ rule in your hearts, since as members of one body you were called to peace. And be thankful.

ABOUT 1 THESSALONIANS

Paul wrote this letter to encourage believers who were being persecuted (treated badly because of their faith). He gives them hope by telling them about the Lord's return. He also gives them practical advice on how to live a life that is pleasing to God.

1 Thessalonians 5:23

May God Himself, the God of peace, sanctify you through and through. May your whole spirit, soul and body be kept blameless at the coming of our Lord Jesus Christ.

ABOUT 2 THESSALONIANS

This is Paul's second letter to the church in Thessalonica. In this letter he wants to clear up confusion about when the Lord would return, and about what happens to those who have already died. Paul tells them that they should be ready at all times to meet Jesus, yet still continue with their daily lives.

2 Thessalonians 3:16

Now may the Lord of peace Himself give you peace at all times and in every way. The Lord be with all of you.

ABOUT 1 TIMOTHY

Paul wrote this letter to his friend Timothy who was a young pastor in the church at Ephesus. Paul gives him some practical advice about setting an example, using his spiritual gift, working hard, teaching truth, and living a godly life of faith.

1 Timothy 4:12
Don't let anyone look down on you because you are young, but set an example for the believers in speech, in conduct, in love, in faith and in purity.

ABOUT 2 TIMOTHY

In this letter, Paul gives Timothy some final instructions. He encourages Timothy to put up with hardship like a soldier; follow God's rules like an athlete; and work hard like a farmer. Paul also cautions Timothy that people will become more and more evil in the last days.

2 Timothy 1:7
For the Spirit God gave us does not make us timid, but gives us power, love and self-discipline.

ABOUT TITUS

Paul writes to Titus in order to help him get the churches on the island of Crete more organized. Paul had left Titus in Crete to bring order in the churches and to oversee the elders (leaders). Paul tells him what is expected of elders and members of the church.

Titus 3:1-2 (NLT)
Remind the believers to submit to the government and its officers. They should be obedient, always ready to do what is good. They must not slander anyone and must avoid quarreling. Instead, they should be gentle and show true humility to everyone.

ABOUT PHILEMON

Philemon was a believer and a friend of Paul. Philemon's slave had run away and was facing punishment for doing so. While on the run, Onesimus the slave also became a believer. Paul writes to Philemon, asking that he forgive Onesimus and welcome him back as a brother.

Philemon 1:4-5

I always thank my God as I remember you in my prayers, because I hear about your love for all His holy people and your faith in the Lord Jesus.

ABOUT HEBREWS

This letter is a warning to Jewish believers who were thinking of abandoning their faith in Christ and, instead, trying to find favor with God by following the Old Testament laws. The writer declares that Christ is greater than the angels, and Moses, and the high priests. He then gives examples of people in the Old Testament who lived by faith.

Hebrews 12:1 (NLT)

Therefore, since we are surrounded by such a huge crowd of witnesses to the life of faith, let us strip off every weight that slows us down, especially the sin that so easily trips us up. And let us run with endurance the race God has set before us.

ABOUT JAMES

James, the brother of Jesus, wrote this letter to teach Christians how to live a life that is pleasing to God, even when hard times come. They should put their faith into action by not only listening to the Word of God, but by doing what it says.

James 1:2-3 (NLT)

Dear brothers and sisters, when troubles of any kind come your way, consider it an opportunity for great joy. For you know that when your faith is tested, your endurance has a chance to grow.

ABOUT 1 PETER

Peter, a disciple of Jesus, wrote this letter with the help of Silas. The letter was written to encourage believers who were being persecuted for the faith. Peter explains the reason for these trials and urges them to live holy lives.

1 Peter 2:9

But you are a chosen people, a royal priesthood, a holy nation, God's special possession, that you may declare the praises of Him who called you out of darkness into His wonderful light.

ABOUT 2 PETER

This is Peter's second letter, written to all believers. Peter, who is near the end of his life, warns believers not to listen to false teachers who twist the Truth of the Gospel. He reminds them that in the last days, people will make fun of believers about the Lord's coming, just like they mocked Noah before the flood.

2 Peter 3:9

The Lord is not slow in keeping His promise, as some understand slowness. Instead He is patient with you, not wanting anyone to perish, but everyone to come to repentance.

ABOUT 1 JOHN

This letter was written by the Apostle John, who was a witness of all the things Jesus said and did. He assures believers that they are truly saved if they obey God, do what is right, love others, have the Spirit living in them, and are no longer in the habit of sinning.

1 John 1:7

But if we walk in the light, as He is in the light, we have fellowship with one another, and the blood of Jesus, His Son, purifies us from all sin.

ABOUT 2 JOHN

John's second letter warns believers against the lies of the devil. He says that the devil uses deceivers to get God's children to doubt the truth, or to confuse them with things that sound like the truth.

2 John 1:8 (NLT)

Watch out that you do not lose what we have worked so hard to achieve. Be diligent so that you receive your full reward.

ABOUT 3 JOHN

John's third letter is to his friend Gaius. He writes about two people: Diotrephes, a bad example in the Church because he loved to be first; and Demetrius, a good example because he lived his life is such a way that everyone spoke well of him.

3 John 1:11 (GNT)

My dear friend, do not imitate what is bad, but imitate what is good. Whoever does good belongs to God; whoever does what is bad has not seen God.

ABOUT JUDE

Jude, the brother of James, wrote this letter to warn believers about those who twist the truth. He also encourages them to remain strong in their faith.

Jude 1:24-25 (NLT)

Now all glory to God, who is able to keep you from falling away and will bring you with great joy into His glorious presence without a single fault. All glory to Him who alone is God, our Savior through Jesus Christ our Lord. All glory, majesty, power, and authority are His before all time, and in the present, and beyond all time! Amen.

ABOUT REVELATION

John wrote this letter to the seven churches in Asia Minor and to all believers. His revelation (a glimpse into the future) came from Jesus Christ and describes what will happen at the end of time. The book of Revelation focuses on the glory of God, and describes the destruction of the devil. The three main groups of people in Revelation are the Church (believers); the Tribes (believing Jews); and the Nations (unbelievers).

Revelation 21:4

He will wipe every tear from their eyes. There will be no more death or mourning or crying or pain, for the old order of things has passed away.

Word Search
Books of the Old Testament

```
R I O L A M E N T A T I O N S E G D U J
E U H X W V U T S S R A Q P O N M L D O
H N T C K D P J I I H G G F E D A E C B
T O P H A M A S S E H G I P J K U A B L
S M F H J L E N A A G A E D Q T H L P C
E O M J O N A F I L B H C L E A S G S H
P L F C E S C M A E M G T R H I O C G K
Z O O G L X E B H I L S O O J Q J L E T
K S U E P H O A W X G N P E D E H H S O
M F P K E J N D S P O B R A H W A A E Z
F O I N F S O W U M J E O L K N B I T S
S G Z V U M I C Y S M B V G O Y A D S E
U N E X O M E G V I R U E J P K K A A L
C O P N I F E Z A P E E R X I C K B I C
I S H U A Z M H R E T O B W L G U O S I
T J A T E P A T M A L H S M E X K A E N
I Q N K I C R S C V Q O G P U B J D L O
V V I C I Y N A H U M W X O M N W K C R
E E A M Q H A I R A H C E Z A P H G C H
L Y H Z G K K I N G S X O D S T O L E C
```

INSTRUCTIONS:
LOOK FOR THE WORDS ON THE LIST. CIRCLE THEM. WORDS MAY BE HIDDEN HORIZONTALLY, VERTICALLY, DIAGONALLY, FORWARDS, OR BACKWARDS.

- GENESIS
- EXODUS
- LEVITICUS
- NUMBERS
- DEUTERONOMY
- JOSHUA
- JUDGES
- RUTH
- SAMUEL
- KINGS
- CHRONICLES
- EZRA
- NEHEMIAH
- ESTHER
- JOB
- PSALMS
- PROVERBS
- ECCLESIASTES
- SONGOFSOLOMON
- ISAIAH
- JEREMIAH
- LAMENTATIONS
- EZEKIEL
- DANIEL
- HOSEA
- JOEL
- AMOS
- OBADIAH
- JONAH
- MICAH
- NAHUM
- HABAKKUK
- ZEPHANIAH
- HAGGAI
- ZECHARIAH
- MALACHI

Word Search
Books of the New Testament

MATTHEW
MARK
LUKE
JOHN
ACTS
ROMANS
FIRSTCORINTHIANS
SECONDCORINTHIANS
GALATIANS

EPHESIANS
PHILIPPIANS
COLOSSIANS
FIRSTTHESSALONIANS
SECONDTHESSALONIANS
FIRSTTIMOTHY
SECONDTIMOTHY
TITUS
PHILEMON

HEBREWS
JAMES
FIRSTPETER
SECONDPETER
FIRSTJOHN
SECONDJOHN
THIRDJOHN
JUDE
REVELATION

QUIZ

Once you have marked the correct answer to a quiz, look for the number on this page matching the quiz number.

In the space above the number, write the letter next to the answer you marked. It's probably best to use a pencil.

```
T_ _     k_ _ _ _ _m     o_        h_ _ _ _n     i_
20 58    69 35 53 82 46   39        29 63 8 50    17

l_ _ _      t_ _ _ _ _ _e         h_ _ _ _n
23 72 34    74 9 43 30 76 18      32 67 36 10

i_       a       f_ _ _d.     W_ _ _      a     m_ _
64       77 3 45             21 7 24           49 15

f_ _ _d     i_,     h_     h_ _     i_       a_ _ _n,
14 59 40    37      57     42 2     68       31 54 26

a_ _     t_ _ _    i_ _    h_ _    j_ _     w_ _ _
25 66    73 1 48   52      33 79   22 65    44 6 62

a_ _     s_ _ _     a_ _     h_    h_ _
28 60    5 38 71    75 12    55    70 4

a_ _     b_ _ _ _t      t_ _ _      f_ _ _ _ _.
16 51    61 11 47 27    81 19 56    78 13 41 80
```

Matthew 13:44